Conflict in the Ozarks

Conflict
IN
THE Ozarks

Hill Folk, Industrialists, and Government in Missouri's Courtois Hills

DAVID BENAC

Truman State University Press

Cover: View of Fishertown, Ozark Land and Lumber Company, photographs, ca.
1900–1920. WHMC-Rolla.

Cover design: Teresa Wheeler
Type: Adobe Garamond Pro © Adobe Systems Inc.; ITC Tiepolo © Adobe Systems Inc.
Printed by: Thomson-Shore, Dexter, Michigan USA

Library of Congress Cataloging-in-Publication Data

Benac, David, 1974-
  Conflict in the Ozarks : hill folk, industrialists, and government in Missouri's
Courtois Hills / David Benac.
    p. cm.
  Including bibliographical references and index.
  ISBN 978-1-935503-12-5 (pbk. : alk. paper)
  1. Mountain people—Missouri—History—19th century. 2. Mountain people—Ozark
Mountains Region—History—19th century. 3. Social conflict—Missouri—History—
19th century. 4. Government, Resistance to—Missouri—History—19th century.
5. Industrialization—Missouri—History—19th century. 6. Missouri Lumber and
Mining Company—History—19th century. 7. Lumber trade—Social aspects—
Missouri—History—19th century. 8. Lumber trade—Environmental aspects—
Missouri—History—19th century. 9. Missouri—Social conditions—19th century.
10. Ozark Mountains Region—Social conditions—19th century. I. Title.
  F472.O9B3 2010
  977.8'03—dc22

                                                                  2010039343

Contents

Figures

Acknowledgments

This book is the culmination of years of hard work during which time I have received the unflagging support of family, friends, colleagues, and many institutions. The staff of several archives, particularly the Western Historical Manuscripts Collections in both Columbia and Rolla as well as the Special Collections and Archives at Missouri State University, were extremely helpful in my pursuit of voluminous records, which all seemed to need to be recalled from remote-storage locations.

Certain colleagues read and commented on sections of the manuscript and provided invaluable comments. Susan Flader did yeoman's work in her willingness to see the early stages of the manuscript through its roughest days. Truman State University Press has also proved a wonderful partner in this process. Barbara Smith-Mandell saw promise in the manuscript and helped in its transformation into the book it is today.

A special thank you goes out to those closest to me who supported me through the years and ultimately made it possible for me to devote the time and energy to this endeavor.

Chapter 1

The Hills and Their Inhabitants

In the late nineteenth century, as the United States moved towards modernization, people throughout the nation turned to their forests as a means of sustenance and of profit. When industrialization swept across the land, it brought a culture of profit, productivity, and punctuality to regions where people had long prided themselves on independence and self-reliance, and had traditionally structured their lives around the changing seasons. The efforts of rural people to create or maintain lifeways based upon patterns of subsistence within the market economy often resulted in visible clashes of worldviews.

The Missouri Ozarks is a predominately rugged region of sinkholes, rivers, cliffs, hills, and forests, with fertile river valleys and scattered high plains. The Courtois Hills, primarily composed of Reynolds, Shannon, and Carter Counties, is one of the most rugged areas within the Ozarks. Within this region, Carter County was representative of the economic, social, and environmental transitions of those counties. Curtis Fletcher Marbut, a soil scientist for the U.S. Bureau of Soils who gained renown as the founder of modern soil science, undertook a study of his native Ozarks in the early twentieth century. He divided the Ozarks into several regions based on soil types. The Courtois Hills fall in an area characterized by stony loams known as Clarksville soil. According to Marbut, "The areas of Clarksville soils are the most thoroughly dissected of any of the important soil areas of the Ozark Dome. There is no smooth upland soil." He continued, "Practically the whole upland ... is too rough for cultivation, except in small areas"[1] (fig. 1). These geological and topographical characteristics of the region created a unique opportunity for settlers and timbermen.

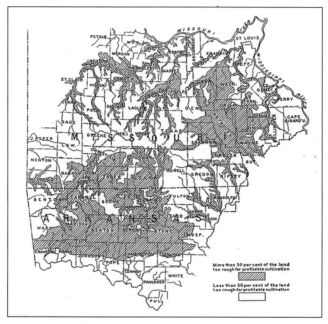

Figure 1: Areas of the Ozarks Too Rugged for Cultivation (Marbut, "Soil Reconnaissance of the Ozark Region," 1732).

Not only was the land terribly rugged, it was also composed of poor soils. Carl O. Sauer, Missouri's most famous geographer, who would become perhaps the most noted geographer of twentieth-century America, beginning with his masterful *Geography of the Ozark Highland* (1920), argued that the high proportion of chert (a rock made up of submicroscopic crystalline silica) in the soils was partially responsible for the shallower and rockier nature of south-facing slopes in comparison to north-facing slopes. Because cherts are excellent conductors of heat and are less mobile than the soils around them, periods of freeze and thaw are more dramatic on sunnier, south-facing slopes. As the

[1] Marbut, "Soil Reconnaissance of the Ozark Region," 1780.

cherts expand and contract, they gradually loosen the surrounding soils and hasten the processes of erosion, leaving the less mobile rocks on the hillsides.

Sauer agreed with Marbut's assessment of the Ozarks. The geographer stated that Clarksville soil constituted "the climax of poverty in the Missouri Ozarks." He argued, "On the whole it contains probably as much chert as any other type of soil, is of lesser depth, and lies on steeper slopes."[2] The combination of rugged topography and poor soils ensured that this portion of the Ozarks would not become a land of large, productive farms. In his detailed study of the lands surrounding the Current River, Donald Stevens explained that in the most difficult hill country, Ozarkers established their homesteads on the banks of the region's rivers, planting small gardens in the most fertile soil. Ozarkers in these valleys then turned to the hillsides as sustenance for their free-range livestock.[3]

Some of the most valuable pine forests of the Missouri Ozarks covered the Courtois Hills, a situation that attracted lumbermen to the region despite its ruggedness (fig. 2).[4] Marbut noted that although much of the Ozark region was interspersed with glades and grassy fields, the Clarksville soil area—that of the Courtois Hills—was heavily timbered. Black oak and shortleaf yellow pine dominated the dry ridgetops and shallow southerly facing slopes. Valleys and the more well-watered north-facing slopes however, were dominated by white and red oaks. Marbut believed that in such an environment, forestry and raising stock would be the only profitable uses of the land.[5]

The ruggedness of the terrain slowed the pace of exploitation, but the valuable shortleaf pine and white oak of this corner of the Missouri Ozarks proved too attractive for timbermen to overlook. The exploitation of the region's forests by lumbermen and Ozarkers created a drastically different forest where shortleaf pine had been the dominant species. Lumbermen had removed the bulk of the region's softwoods by the 1910s, including the mature trees necessary to broadcast seeds for reproduction. Fire and grazing

[2] Sauer, *Geography of the Ozark Highland*, 38.

[3] Stevens, *A Homeland and A Hinterland*, 27; and Marbut, "Physical Features of Missouri."

[4] Krusekopf, *Soil Survey of Reynolds County, Missouri*, 3–4.

[5] Marbut, "Soil Reconnaissance of the Ozark Region," 1738, 1746, 1781; and Sauer, *Geography of the Ozark Highland*, 41, 56–58.

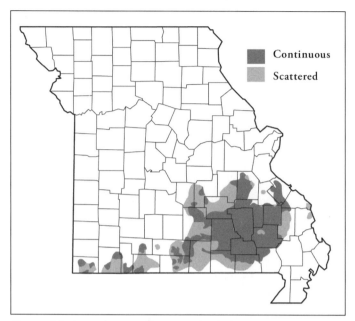

Figure 2: The Original Extent of Missouri's Shortleaf Pine Forests (Lawrence, Moltzan, and Moser, "Oak Decline and the Future of Missouri's Forests," 3).

then kept new pine seedlings from getting a start, enabling fire-resistant hard-woods with the ability to stump sprout to take over the forests.[6]

Carter County has a central place in this story because it hosted the larg-est timber operation in the Ozarks and demonstrated many of the social, eco-nomic, and political issues of the surrounding Courtois Hills. As the center of the Ozark timber boom, Carter County (figs. 3–4) vividly portrays the social and environmental changes surrounding the growth and collapse of the industry, as well as the increasing presence of government in distinct portions of the Ozarks. After the timber boom and coincident with the rise of conser-vationist sentiment in Missouri, the forests and cutover lands of the region claimed the attention of sportsmen, reformers, and government agents.

[6] Cunningham and Hauser, "Decline of the Missouri Ozark Forest," 181–82; and Sauer, *Geography of the Ozark Highland.*

Figure 3: Missouri Counties (U.S. Census Bureau, Census 2000).

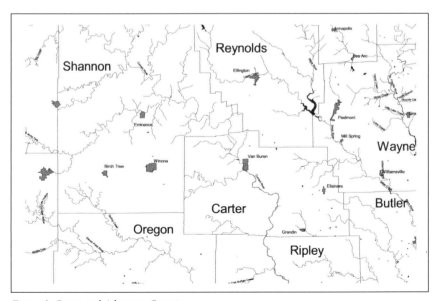

Figure 4: Carter and Adjoining Counties.

The Forest-Subsistence Society

The first white settlers to the region that would become Carter County established homesteads on land where they enjoyed a lifestyle similar to that of their ancestors, who had made their homes in the upland South. These new Ozarkers began to arrive in the 1820s and chose locations along the rivers flowing between Missouri and Arkansas.[7] Many of the immigrants to the Courtois Hills were of Scottish descent and entered Missouri from the Appalachians in kin groups, as demonstrated by census returns. These newcomers from Tennessee and Kentucky were often unable to purchase large tracts of land and, as a result, viewed the woods as a commons available for the subsistence needs of all.[8]

Several of the founding families in the area illustrate this heritage. Zimri Carter, the county's namesake, moved to the present site of Van Buren in 1812 or 1813 after leaving South Carolina, his residence since birth in 1794. Reverend George Sumner's parents moved from Tennessee to the banks of the Current River, where he was born in 1847. James Norton, born in Kentucky in 1839, moved to Shannon County in 1858 after a short stay in Audrain County, Missouri.[9] The rugged hills offered an attractive destination for upland southerners looking for new lands.

Because it was such difficult land, most of the Courtois Hills did not see substantial white settlement until federal programs made marginal lands more desirable in the 1850s. In 1854, the federal government passed the Graduation Act to speed the settlement of poor agricultural lands nationwide. The act gradually lowered the price of public land in a series of steps to a minimum of twelve and one half cents per acre for land that remained unpurchased for thirty years. Although the federal government envisioned this procedure as a reward for farmers with limited capital but ample ambition, it resulted in a great deal of land speculation. Throughout the most rugged areas of the Ozarks, including the Courtois Hills, individuals took advantage of the Graduation Act and rapidly purchased available land.[10]

---

[7] Gerlach, *Settlement Patterns in Missouri*, 19.

[8] Gerlach, *Settlement Patterns in Missouri*, 22–23, 28, 55, 71, 74; and Gibson, "Living by the Land," 23–24.

[9] *Reminiscent History of the Ozarks Region*, 457–58, 664–65, 752–53. This anonymous work offers a colorful and apparently solid account of the early days of the region. Census records corroborate the factual accounts contained in the work.

[10] Gibson, "Living by the Land," 24–25. Land records confirm an increasing volume of sales, especially

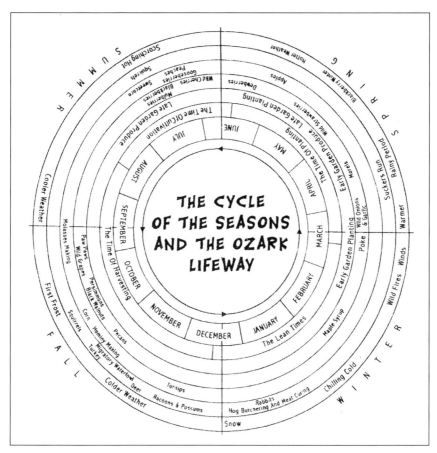

Figure 5: Seasonality of Ozarkers' Woods Use (Jim Price, "Ozark Experiences").

Before the arrival of the large-scale timber industry, a forest-subsistence economy existed in parts of the Ozarks where residents molded their lives around the changing seasons (fig. 5). During winter when crops planted along river bottoms and wild flora were not available, these individuals hunted and trapped small game to survive. To supply their families with meat for the upcoming months, these hill folk also used the cold weather to their advantage by butchering and curing free-range hogs they rounded up from the nearby woods.

---

of larger tracts of land after 1854.

As the cold weather broke and fires ripped through the woods, those who depended on the forest for subsistence could see the beginning of easier times. Early spring brought the first edible plants and herbs to the woods and marked the time to plant gardens and small amounts of sweet corn and wheat. During summer and fall, the woods produced berries and gardens began to provide a wealth of vegetables, most notably sweet corn, leading to the busiest portion of the year in the pre-industrial Courtois Hills. By the end of summer, locals shifted much of their diet to game animals and harvested the remainder of their corn and the foodstuffs of the woods. Through generations of exploiting the hill country, forest-subsistence Ozarkers established a pattern of life based on the seasonal bounty of the land.

Woods-burning was a tool many Ozarkers used to modify the hillsides to meet their needs. Ashley Schiff, who studied the U.S. Forest Service's relationship with fire, sought out the origins of woods-burning. He determined that

> Dating back to the settlement of the coastal-plain flatwoods three hundred years ago, man had used fire initially to clear ground for farming and then to provide improved winter pasture for his livestock. He had observed that animals fared better on a fresh burn which destroyed the mat of dead grass, needles, and litter suppressing new growth. Migrating pioneers carried this custom into the Piedmont uplands and the Appalachian, Arkansas, and Missouri mountains.

Schiff went on to point out that many woods-burners considered the practice proof against snakes and ticks as well as invaluable in manipulating the woods so cattle could be found on the open range.[11] The strong commitment to the value of fire among many residents of the Courtois Hills would emerge as one of the most consistent and significant areas of conflict between Ozarkers and government.

---

[11] Schiff, *Fire and Water*, 17–18.

Changes in the Hills

Those individuals who chose to make one of the most rugged portions of the Ozarks their home reacted to changes in the environmental, economic, and social conditions surrounding their lives at the community and individual levels. This book is not an attempt to extrapolate the behaviors of a selected group of Ozarkers to represent hill folk as a whole. Following in the well-established footprints of historians of Appalachia, historians of the Ozarks have recently concentrated on the image of the Ozarker in the popular imagination and broad studies of the region as a whole. This region—the Courtois Hills—is a unique and dramatically overlooked area of the Missouri Ozarks.

There are several pertinent questions to consider. What events encouraged the growth of large-scale timber production in the Missouri Ozarks? How did the timber industry operate alongside the existing economies of the region? How did inhabitants of the Courtois Hills participate in the industrial harvest of timber? What did those who chose to remain in the region after the mills closed turn to for subsistence? How did the experiences of the residents in the hill country affect their interactions with governmental agents and conservationists? Many of the answers to these questions lie within the framework of recent environmental history that examines how society, culture, and economic strategy interact with the environment.

The story of the shaping of the forests and society in the most rugged portions of the Missouri Ozarks is an illuminating study of the evolution of the state's relationships with its woodlands. The growth of the industrial economy and governmental involvement in the Courtois Hills led to a series of changes in the economy, culture, and politics of those who chose to live in the region, as well as a constant re-evaluation among Missourians as to the importance of woodlands in the state. Between approximately 1880 and 1950, a series of events caused these changes to play out in visible ways.

In the struggle for control of the region's forests, residents of the hills, industrialists, and government agents created environmental and social changes. Each desired to determine the woodlands' use and place in society. Those residents who preceded industrialization had created a forest-subsistence economy dependent on the woodlands for nuts, berries, herbs, game animals, fodder for livestock, and wood for warmth, cooking, and for building homes and fences. Industrialists entered the region with a view of forests as warehouses of raw materials for sawmills that would produce lumber for distant markets. As industrialists established a foothold in the Courtois Hills, longtime residents of the region often joined the market economy by selling timber, ties, and stumpage to industrialists.[12] At the same time, these preindustrial residents held on to some of their older ideals, patterns of behavior that some newcomers embraced as well.

Much of the upheaval in the region beginning in the second half of the nineteenth century was a result of conflicts over cultural control. As timber companies moved into the region, they established new schools, churches, libraries, social associations, newspapers, railroads, company stores, and other institutions under their control. These new institutions, in part, displaced their existing counterparts. This interplay between new and older institutions and the individuals who supported them is a large component of the story of life in the Courtois Hills in the second half of the nineteenth century.

The evolution of the relationship between residents of the Courtois Hills and their forests did not stop with the timber industry. Governmental efforts and the birth of the conservation movement drastically shifted the way all Missourians viewed the land. Forest management and conservation in Missouri applied most directly to the Ozarks and with special immediacy to the heavily cutover region of the Courtois Hills. To fully understand the implications of the actions of the timber companies and new residents to the region it is important to consider what happened when new forces stepped into the picture in the Missouri forests.

Arrival of Industry

The large-scale timber industry came to the Missouri Ozarks in the 1880s and grew until it peaked around 1899 to 1900. The largest company was the Missouri Lumber and Mining Company (MLM), which built its first mill in 1880. Although this first effort failed for a lack of railroad connections, the company continued its interest in the area and succeeded in establishing a more permanent presence in Carter County at Grandin, a company town the MLM founded in 1884. Two other large timber concerns operated in the area contemporaneously with the MLM, the Cordz-Fisher Lumber Company in

---

[12] The sale of "stumpage" occurs when a landowner sells the right to cut standing timber.

Birch Tree and the Ozark Land and Lumber Company in Winona, both in Shannon County. The MLM serves as the center of this study because it was by far the largest of the three and has left extensive records.[13]

From the forest industry's first days in the region, Ozarkers accepted its new economic and social patterns with varying degrees of eagerness. Locals accepted jobs in the mills and logging camps, and supplied the operations with timber and ties from their own lands, taking advantage of the opportunities of the market economy. In the process of adapting to the new economy, residents of the mill towns and hills, whether newcomers or long-established, often clashed with the industrial leadership. Employees and contractors attempted to control the pace and hours of work, the occasion of holidays, the education their children received, the shape of religious beliefs, and opportunities for, and use of, leisure time. Industrial leadership was most concerned with productivity, but did not yield its Victorian ideals of social and cultural actions to employees' desires. The divergent attitudes on economic, social, and cultural development resulted in a series of clashes and compromises throughout the industrial era.[14]

The Role of Government

The state and federal governments were slow to make significant attempts to gain control of the Ozark forests. The Courtois Hills provide an opportunity for detailed study, as the region was central to almost every stage of state and federal efforts regarding forest policy in Missouri. The state's first broadly conceived conservation efforts emerged out of a movement by sportsmen to maintain viable game populations, a group and issue the state would never abandon as it attempted to establish natural resource policies. Governmental involvement with Missouri's forests, however, began with close relationships to the timber industry. Industrialists' attempts to seize and maintain control

[13] The company's records are held by Western Historical Manuscripts Collection at Ellis Library in Columbia, MO, and labeled as the Missouri Lumber and Mining Company Records, 1853–1945. The collection consists of 7109 folders, 194 volumes, and 3 rolls of microfilm. Hereafter the collection is cited as MLM Records.

[14] For examples of workers in other areas of the United States attempting to gain control of their workplaces, see Montgomery, *Workers' Control in America*; and Janiewski, "Southern Honor, Southern Dishonor."

of conservation effectively kept government out of conservation in the Courtois Hills until well into the 1930s.

By the 1920s, the activities of timber companies and farmers had left the most rugged areas of the Ozarks with a dramatically reduced forest resource, resulting in subsequent depression. Whether acting out of altruism, in an effort to extend their influence, or in response to prodding by industrialists, the state and federal governments recognized the dire situation and began to propose several programs to repair the region's environmental and economic damages. Missouri's game wardens and foresters acted to improve the common good as they saw it, even when that belief conflicted with residents of the region to be managed.

The federal government's earliest involvement in Missouri's forests was essentially limited to providing the state with funds for conservation. Once the U.S. Congress passed the Clarke-McNary Act in 1924, the federal government had the authority to provide funds to states for forestry, if the states met certain qualifications. Despite this opportunity, Missouri would not participate in federal forestry until the early 1930s, when the state legislature passed an enabling act to allow the federal government to purchase land for national forests within its borders. The state's decision to participate in federal forestry made it eligible to take advantage of the economic opportunities such involvement presented. Although this legislation opened Missouri to the U.S. Forest Service, it limited the number of acres the federal government could purchase in each county to a number that was too small for efficient management. In the mid-1930s, Missourians finally released these acreage restrictions and the federal government claimed a new role in the Missouri Ozarks by purchasing the lands that would become the Mark Twain National Forest.[15]

In 1936, Missouri responded to a campaign led by sportsmen and passed a constitutional amendment to create a conservation commission through statewide election. The commission then hired its first state forester in 1938. Even with the new agency, the state and federal governments continued to deal with the same difficulties they had faced for two decades: fire and open-range grazing. Both the state and federal forestry agencies devoted the bulk of their efforts to controlling and preventing forest fires, but they had little success until well

[15] Keefe, *First 50 Years*, 202–3.

into the 1940s. Residents of large sections of the Ozarks continued to burn the woods with some regularity and to graze cattle on the open range, which Missouri did not end statewide until 1969. The combination of fire and grazing left forests such as those in the Courtois Hills impoverished and unable to support extensive use.

Questions and Sources

A number of significant questions call out for attention. How did Missouri fit within the national context of the timber industry? What kind of timber did the industry utilize? Who worked in the logging camps and the mills? What was the role of railroads? How did the lives of employees and contractors change and how did those individuals deal with those changes? How did timbermen and hill folk who remained in the region after the timber boom cope? How and when did the state and federal governments attempt to intervene in the region with conservation and social aid, and how did governmental agents and programs overcome local resistance?

The extensive records of the MLM, in conjunction with the records of other companies, proved to be one of the most complete sources of information for answering many of these questions. These records trace the rise and fall of the timber industry in Missouri between 1880 and 1910. As the main company in this study, the MLM takes a central role; its records reveal not only the daily processes of its operation, but also its creation and governance of the community of Grandin. Even after many of the state's large timber operations left for greener pastures, the records of those who remained to exploit hardwoods for railroad ties and cooperage stock provide great insight into their operations.

Oral histories and local newspapers give voice to those residents of the region who left few records. Newspapers, such as the Grandin *Herald*, which Elbert C. White published as a Republican weekly from October 1905 through at least mid-1909, covered the actions of timber companies and their employees in detail, often operating in close cooperation with the companies they discussed.[16] Although it was an economically independent entity, the

---

[16] Despite the shared surname, there is no indication of a familial relationship between Elbert White and John Barber White.

Herald maintained a close relationship with the MLM throughout its existence. The evidence in these sources shines light on the resistance many residents offered when timber companies attempted to gain control over society in several arenas, including Sunday labor, violence, and the use of alcohol.

Governmental documents provide statistical data on the extent of Missouri's forests, the incidence of fires, and the status of agencies and legislation. They are also crucial in understanding how governmental agencies achieved several victories for management over natural resources in the region during the 1930s and 1940s, despite never obtaining complete control.

Ultimately, the story of the Courtois Hills and the contest for control of the region's natural and social resources has implications beyond even the Missouri Ozarks. Many of the issues addressed by employers, employees, and governmental agencies in the Courtois Hills are still contested in resource-dependent communities throughout the United States and the world.

Historiographical Context

This is not a grand synthesis of Ozark history. There is ample historiographical tradition to illustrate the danger of generalizing about the whole from any constituent part. The series of issues that took place in the circumscribed area discussed herein hold the potential to further our knowledge of Ozark history. Many of the conclusions presented fly in the face of recent scholarship. Because of their ruggedness and difficult terrain, the Courtois Hills sit as an intriguing subregion with their own history—one that may inspire much discussion.

The pool of research done on the Ozarks is relatively shallow compared with areas bearing similar characteristics, such as the Appalachians. What this pool lacks in depth, it makes up for in breadth. Historians, folklorists, novelists, geographers, sociologists, and a host of other authors have all approached the Ozarks from insightful angles in the past three-quarters of a century. A number of somewhat dated sources provided invaluable discussions of the region as a whole. Otto Ernest Rayburn, an Ozarker, writer, and regional booster, first brought the Ozarks into the national consciousness with *Ozark Country* (1941). In *Bittersweet Country* (1978), Ellen Gray Massey, much like Rayburn, investigated pre-industrial life in the Ozarks with an emphasis on the people who chose to locate to and remain in the hills. Not all of the early work on the region was solely cultural. The geographer Milton D. Rafferty drew on a wide variety of sources to create a historical geography of the region with *The Ozarks: Land and Life* (1980). He created a general overview of the environment and the history of the region, but he did not find it within his purview to analyze the significance of social changes in the hill country.

The issue of conservation is one that has served as an important tool for evaluating the Ozarks since the mid-twentieth century. Charles Callison, in *Man and Wildlife in Missouri* (1953), and James F. Keefe, in *The First 50 Years* (1987), each investigate the relationship of Ozarkers to their forests and to the conservation movement. Both Callison and Keefe saw the issues of forest conservation as part of a larger context of fish and game conservation.

In recent years, the literature addressing the history of the Ozarks has grown, yet in many ways continues to follow trends in the study of the Appalachians. Historians of Appalachia have wrestled with many of the same issues historians of the Ozarks regularly confront. Appalachian history, a discipline several decades more established than Ozarks history, provides important guideposts. In *Appalachia in the Making*, Mary Beth Pudup, Dwight Billings, and Altina Waller pull together an important and wide range of essays. The authors of these articles demand a more nuanced understanding of the region, exploring race, gender, and the nature of capitalism. The authors argue that the residents of the hills were active in the broad sweep of history, not the isolated and backward folk of myth. John Alexander Williams, in *Appalachia: A History* (2002), compiles a massive historical account investigating the intertwined nature of Appalachian and American history. Williams paints a complex picture of the Appalachian region.

This more nuanced approach has made important contributions to studies of Ozarks history. Kathleen Morrison turned to a strictly economic analysis to discuss the development of the Ozarks. In "The Poverty of Place" (1999), she created an economic and geographic analysis of how highway connections created pockets of local affluence and concluded that the region's poverty is directly related to its remote location. Morrison's discoveries mirror the situation in the Courtois Hills. In the same year, Lynn Morrow released *Shepherd of the Hills: Tourism Transforms the Ozarks, 1880s–1930s* (1999). In his excellent study of the economics of the region, Morrow discusses the timber industry and other sources of income with a focus on the dramatic impact of the tourism industry. Tourism has continued to gain in economic importance throughout the Ozarks and today it is the largest source of income for the Courtois Hills.

Brooks Blevins, *Hill Folks: A History of Arkansas Ozarkers and Their Image* (2001), labors to reshape our understanding of Ozarkers. He follows the pattern of Appalachian history that demands a closer and more nuanced accounting of local variation and places hill folks within the modern and capitalistic system. Blevins carefully studies the region's history, but in his efforts to demonstrate that these distinct histories meshed closely with larger national histories, he fails to acknowledge the largely isolated history of the Courtois Hills.

In contrast to Blevins's work, Bonnie Stepenoff, *Big Spring Autumn* (2008), selects the Courtois Hills for detailed treatment. She is one of the few authors to have attempted a study of this difficult region. Stepenoff's lively work hints at the historically important economic and social issues of the area, while offering insightful environmental observations.

What remains and follows is the outgrowth of years of scholarship and study. It is important as historians seek to understand the Ozarks that the complexity of the interrelationships between various communities of people and the natural environment all appear in the discussion. It is also time that historians recognize that subregions within the Ozarks existed and developed in disparate ways and that their study will help with understanding the region as a whole.

Chapter 2

The Missouri Lumber and Mining Company and the Timber Industry

Despite a long history of dependence on their forests, southern Missourians developed no significant timber industry until the late 1880s. This industrial lumbering in Missouri coincided with the simultaneous decline of the pineries farther east and in the Great Lakes states. By the early 1880s, railroads, largely under subsidiary branches of the Kansas City, Fort Scott, and Memphis Railroad, had begun to open areas of the Ozarks where valuable shortleaf pine dominated open forests with significant populations of other species such as white and red oak. The new mode of transportation provided industrialists access to markets, labor, and machinery from a network that covered most of the country and made exploitation of the forests of the rugged Ozarks possible. Timbermen from the East who had begun buying land in the region more than a decade earlier brought industry to the hill country and rapidly worked to consolidate and create economies of scale in the Missouri Ozarks.

Before large-scale timbering began, the wooded sections of the Missouri Ozarks were dominated by open forests of large trees and sparse undergrowth, interspersed with areas of prairie and meadows. After decades of analyzing the species composition of Missouri's forests, Julian A. Steyermark published his

Vegetational History of the Ozark Forests in 1959. Comparing the results of his studies with the original land surveys of the region, Steyermark found that the Ozark forests had been composed of a variable mix of pine and oak for millennia, explaining that "certain species of plants favored the exposed limestone strata, while others took to the more acidic cherts, sandstones, and igneous granites." Based on this geological understanding of the forests, Steyermark argued that oaks dominated richer soils throughout the Ozarks, while yellow pine was the dominant species on hillsides, ridges, and bluffs where the soils had become acidic through the natural processes of erosion.[1] These conclusions closely mirrored the findings of Curtis F. Marbut, who had studied the Ozarks fifty years earlier.[2] The Ozark forests presented settlers, and later businessmen, with a rich forest full of opportunities and challenges.

The earliest white American settlers in the Courtois Hills followed a trend of Europeans moving ever farther into the backcountry. Though the French had settled the fringes of the region, it was not until the decade after the Louisiana Purchase that the first Europeans (now Americans) settled the interior of the Ozarks. These recent arrivals looking to stay on the outer edge of American settlement brought with them the traditions their ancestors had honed in the backcountry of the upland South. The continuity of traditions carried from the hillcountry of the Carolinas, Kentucky, and Tennessee to the Missouri Ozarks shaped much of the history of the Courtois Hills. Faced with a woodland of imposing proportions, these new Ozarkers utilized and shaped their surroundings in well-established ways to meet their needs and desires. From their earliest days in the region, white settlers burned the woods each spring for their livestock and used trees to build and heat their homes.

Missourians recognized the value of the Ozark forests in the first years of the nineteenth century, but those forests were generally located on rough terrain far removed from efficient transportation. Early timbering in the Missouri Ozarks was restricted to the immediate vicinity of waterways large enough to support log drives, such as the Gasconade River, which flows into the Missouri River and connects to the Mississippi at St. Louis. Timbermen

---

[1] Steyermark, *Vegetational History of the Ozark Forest*, 64, 111.

[2] Marbut, "Physical Features of Missouri," 15; and Marbut, "Soil Reconnaissance of the Ozark Region," 1780.

began to harvest the lands along that river in 1818; by 1852, they had cut all accessible timber in that area and softwoods, especially shortleaf pine, dominated the output of the mills. The difficult terrain of the Courtois Hills prevented timbermen from more fully exploiting the area's resources during this early era of the industry. In the second half of the century, a significant change occurred when railroads opened the most rugged portions of the Ozarks and provided inexpensive and dependable transportation to outside markets.

Even before the railroads opened up the region, outside speculators began to take notice of the economic possibilities in the hill country and tried to acquire land, usually without fully revealing their intentions. In December 1871, arsonists burned the courthouses in Reynolds and Shannon Counties. The editor of the Iron County *Register* speculated that the fires, which destroyed almost all records, had been set to cover the actions of a land-fraud ring. He proposed, "A little 'lynch law' even, would not be entirely out of place, in case of certainty." After nearly four years of investigation, authorities indicted three St. Louis residents for forging deeds to sell land in Shannon County.[3] The presence of a market for forged land deeds to some of the most rugged property in the Ozarks marked a growing interest in the region.

O. H. P. Williams, a Pittsburgh lumberman, and his son-in-law E. B. Grandin, an oil magnate from Tidouite, Pennsylvania, learned of the valuable timber in Missouri's Courtois Hills in the mid-nineteenth century. By the close of the 1860s, the two men had made their initial purchases in the region in northeast Ripley County. Less than a decade later, the two men returned, and this time purchased more than 30,000 acres in Carter County. In 1880, these men joined with J. L. Grandin and Jahu Hunter, also of Tidouite, to form the Missouri Lumber and Mining Company (MLM).[4] As with many timber companies of the late nineteenth century, the MLM began as a group of investors from the East with interests in the forests of the West. John Barber White was the only initial company executive to leave Pennsylvania to live in Missouri. As the general manager, White assumed the most active role in the MLM's daily activities.[5]

---

[3] Iron County *Register*, 2 December 1871; 13 January 1872; and 9 December 1875.

[4] Hill, "History of the Missouri Lumber and Mining Company," 10–13.

[5] J. B. White to the company's board of directors, 26 December 1905, folder 49, MLM Records.

The Arrival of the Missouri Lumber and Mining Company

The MLM constructed its initial mill along the Black River, near present-day Williamsville, in Wayne County on the northeast border of Carter County, and named it White's Mill after John Barber White. This mill consisted of both a sawing and a planing operation. Transportation was a persistent problem for White's Mill; though the mill could turn out as much as six million board feet of lumber per year, it still relied on a ten-mile oxcart connection to the nearest railroad spur.

Throughout the years it operated White's Mill the MLM continually sought a close relationship with railroads, a management strategy that would characterize much of the company's development. As early as 1882, the company worked to form an alliance with the Kansas City, Fort Scott, and Memphis Railroad (KFS&M), which had just completed a line from Springfield to Thayer, Missouri, on the Arkansas border to the south and west of the site that would become the town of Grandin. Despite these efforts, the MLM closed White's Mill in 1884 because of its failure to obtain a railroad connection to transport logs and lumber. At the time the mill closed, the company owned approximately 100,000 acres of timberland in Carter County alone.[6]

After this initial failure, the MLM moved its operation southwest to a vacant location near the Current River previously known as Tolliver's Pond. The MLM obtained the pond and about eighty adjacent acres, and named the newly platted town Grandin. By 1887, the company had reached an agreement with the KFS&M Railroad whereby the timber company guaranteed a minimum amount of traffic and the railroad built an eighty-one-mile line from Willow Springs, a location on the original line, to the proposed location of Grandin. This railroad incorporated as the Current River Railroad and arrived in Grandin in the summer of 1889 to find a yard full of lumber awaiting shipment.[7] Later in 1889, the Cape Girardeau Southwestern Railroad met the Current River Railroad's line in Hunter, Missouri, offering the MLM access to eastern markets to supplement their connection to the West.[8]

---

[6] Hill, "History of the Missouri Lumber and Mining Company," 21–23, 27; and Collection cover sheet, folder 1, MLM Records.

[7] Galloway, "John Barber White," 27–28; and Hill, "History of the Missouri Lumber and Mining Company," 29–31.

[8] Stevens, *A Homeland and A Hinterland*, 75; and Hill, "History of the Missouri Lumber and Mining

Figure 6: "Log Train" (folder 1, p. 11, MLM Company Photographs, 1906–1916, WHMC–Columbia).

The railroad immediately became a crucial component of the MLM's operations. In 1897 White demonstrated the company's commitment to railroad transport when he reported to an official of the Union Pacific Railroad that the MLM and its allied companies owned one hundred miles of rail lines.[9] The increasing mileage of railroads thoughout the Ozarks proved invaluable as the MLM and other large timber companies exploited the region's forests (see fig. 6).[10]

The MLM and other companies struggled to purchase enough timberlands, stumpage, and logs at profitable prices to maintain a viable industry in the Courtois Hills. Once local residents realized the extent of the company's

Company," 31–33.

[9] J. B. White to H. G. Kaill, 13 August 1897, folder 1, MLM Records.

[10] For visual representations of railroads in Missouri, see "Cram's Railroads and Townships of Missouri" (Chicago: Geo. T. Cram, 1874), collection no. 783; and "Commissioners' Official Railway Map of Missouri" (1 January 1888), collection no. 2444. Both maps are at WHMC.

need for good woodland, however, land prices skyrocketed. The MLM also had to sort through unsolicited offers for timber too distant from transportation to be of value.[11] White and his chief clerk and sales agent, C. C. Sheppard (a local man), selected land for purchase based on the value of its timber and its distance from rail or river transportation. When W. B. Pettibone offered a parcel to the MLM, White rejected the proposal because the land was "at least eight miles from the Current River" and "on the opposite side of the river from where we are building our railroad."[12] An overland distance of a mere eight miles was too far to transport logs because, as one of the company's teamsters said, "this land is all terrible rough."[13]

Despite the opportunities railroads presented to the MLM, the new transportation systems also created a series of challenges. One difficulty was the necessary investment. Historian James E. Fickle noted that it cost approximately one thousand dollars per mile of track to build logging railroads in Mississippi.[14] With similar technology available and an environmental and topographical situation that posed at least as many challenges, it is doubtful that Missouri's timbermen spent any less to build their railroads. Another difficulty of rail transportation was maintaining and operating the necessary miles of track. To maintain an effective rail system and keep raw timber and finished products moving, the MLM employed 250 men strictly for railroad work.[15] Timber companies also faced environmental difficulties such as heavy rains and floods, which washed out bridges on several occasions (see fig. 7).[16]

Although railroads proved indispensable for the MLM, the company also continued to utilize log drives via the region's waterways. The ruggedness of the Courtois Hills prevented timber and railroad companies from building rail lines in many areas. Where the land proved unsuitable for rails but possessed valuable timber, industrialists often hired locals to harvest the trees and

[11] J. B. White to W. B. Pettibone, no date, folder 57, MLM Records.

[12] J. B. White to W. B. Pettibone, no date, folder 57, MLM Records. Pettibone's position in the area is uncertain. A man of the appropriate age appears as a resident of northeast Missouri as early as 1880, with a birthplace in Wisconsin, but left no record of ever living in the Grandin area (see census records).

[13] Alex Carter to J. B. White, 19 July 1904, folder 4, MLM Records.

[14] Fickle, *Mississippi Forests and Forestry*, 78.

[15] Ponder, *Grandin, Hunter, and West Eminence*, 15.

[16] Grandin *Herald*, 22 November 1906.

Figure 7: "Washed Out Railroad Bridge" (folder 1, p. 22a, MLM Company Photographs, 1906-1916, WHMC–Columbia).

float the logs to the mills. River drives served a minor position in the industry, however, because of the difficulties posed by droughts, floods, ice, and the average pace of only about one mile per day. Log drives were dangerous and inefficient, but the industry used them when rivers were the only means of extracting valuable timber from the hills.[17]

When the large-scale timber industry entered the Ozarks in the late nineteenth century, locals encountered a challenge to their previous relationship with the woods. Between 1860 and 1870, the population of Carter County grew from a mere 1,234 people to a still-small number of 1,455 (fig. 8).[18] This increase of 221 people raised the population density of the county to approximately two people per square mile (Carter County's area is 688 square miles) by 1870. Although settlement was concentrated along river valleys, the sparse population of the region ensured that these hill folk would retain close-knit relationships with a small number of people, isolated from outside economic and cultural influences. Another significant element of the low

---

[17] Cunningham, "River Drives," 3; and Grandin *Herald*, 26 July 1906.

[18] Stevens, *A Homeland and A Hinterland*, 96.

Figure 8: Population of Carter County, Johnson Township, and Grandin, 1870–1960.

Year	Carter County	Johnson Township	Grandin[19]
1870	1,455		
1880	2,168	516	
1890	4,659	1,806	579
1900	6,706	2,953	3,000
1910	5,504	2,025	
1920	7,482	2,140	
1930	5,503	1,783	309
1940	6,226	1,986	294
1950	4,773	1,481	263
1960	3,973	1,417	259

SOURCES: U.S. Censuses, 1870–1960; McManus, *Grandin (Carter) Missouri Records*; Denney, *Regional Profile of the Ozark Foothills*; Ensminger, "Handbook for Community Organizers"; Oakley, *History of Grandin*; Oakley, *Deserted Village*; *Missouri State Gazetteer and Business Directory* for 1893–1894; and *Missouri State Gazetteer* for 1898–1899.

population density was the land's ability to sustain residents' seasonal patterns of woodland exploitation.

Life changed drastically when industrialists moved into the region with a view of forests as resources to be turned into financial profit.[20] Population pressure intensified at the same time that the MLM and other companies in the region began to dramatically alter the forests of the Ozarks. By 1880, the population of Carter County had climbed to 2,168 and reached 4,659 by 1890.[21] When the MLM shut down White's Mill in 1884, the company was

[19] Grandin, which is in Johnson Township, disappeared from U.S. Census records between 1890 and 1930. The only available population estimate for the period (3,000 in 1900) was provided by Eugene Oakley, a local historian in Carter County. There seems to be some basis for this number, despite its being higher than the census taker's count for the entire township. Leslie Hill notes that the company had more than 1,000 employees in 1900 and 1,500 by 1905. Based on these figures, a population of 3,000 in 1900 is reasonable.

[20] For a similar episode of the conflict between corporate and communal rights to resources, see Kulik, "Dams, Fish, and Farmers."

[21] Stevens, *A Homeland and A Hinterland*, 96.

employing 125 men at the site.[22] By 1890, just three years after the company set up its mill in Grandin, the population density in Carter County reached a little over six and one half people per square mile.

Rationalization of the Industry

J. B. White worked diligently to establish himself as the regional leader in an efficiently structured timber industry. As early as 1882, he made efforts to stabilize the industry in Missouri by pooling the resources of competing corporations. Other timbermen in the region were not as eager to enter into alliances and showed little support for these first attempts. By 1890, however, White had gained the backing of enough of his contemporaries to become president of the brand new Southern Lumber Manufacturers' Association. This new association created uniform grading regulations and cooperative price lists, and attempted to get better railroad rates for its members.[23] Throughout his career, White worked to reduce what he saw as unnecessary competition and to increase the efficiency and profitability of the timber industry in Missouri and throughout the South.

His efforts to rationalize the region's timber industry really took off when he moved his offices in 1891 to Kansas City, into the same building as the Cordz-Fisher Lumber Company, the Ozark Land and Lumber Company, and the smaller Holladay-Klotz Land and Lumber Company.[24] Once he settled in, White encouraged these neighboring corporations to unite with the MLM to create a potential industry juggernaut, the Missouri Land and Lumber Exchange. This association was designed to serve as a clearinghouse for resources (whether timber, land, or labor) and products for the benefit of all members. The exchange increased White's position among the nation's lumbermen and gave him a platform from which to oversee prices and production for Missouri's and, later, Louisiana's mills.[25] White operated within a historical context in which consolidation characterized the development of business structures throughout the nation.[26]

---

[22] Galloway, "John Barber White," 27.

[23] Galloway, "John Barber White," 103–5.

[24] Hill, "History of the Missouri Lumber and Mining Company," 94.

[25] Galloway, "John Barber White," 68–77.

[26] For one treatment of consolidation in business, see Chandler, *Visible Hand*.

The importance of White and the MLM was obvious in the organization of the exchange. Before the members decided to incorporate, they agreed to a trial run where they assigned sales to each of the companies based on their production capacities. The MLM would account for 50 percent of all sales, Ozark Lumber, 27 percent; Cordz-Fisher, 13 percent; and Holladay-Klotz, 10 percent. After four months of this trial arrangement, the actual values each company produced differed slightly from the goal. The MLM did just over 42 percent of the exchange's business, while the others handled 36 percent, 14 percent, and 6 percent, respectively.[27] When the exchange incorporated, White accepted the MLM's slightly reduced role in order to introduce a force for stability into the marketplace, but Holladay-Klotz believed it could do better on its own and remained independent. The participating members— the MLM, Ozark Lumber, and Cordz-Fisher—divided the exchange's business at 50 percent, 30 percent, and 20 percent, respectively.[28] The exchange demonstrates White's efforts to create and control an exceptionally well-organized and large-scale industry, almost from his first days in Missouri.

From its inception, the exchange placed White in a powerful position, which he recognized. In 1897, he wrote to J. H. Berkshire, a representative of Ozark Lumber, to propose that the exchange increase prices by one or two cents at various points in the manufacture of timber to offset losses in other aspects of production. White explained: "I think this plan is strictly honest, and is a plan that is followed by all of the coal dealers, and by the Standard Oil Co., and I think all are large commercial shippers."[29] Four years later, White received a letter from a Wisconsin man interested in purchasing land from one of the companies in Louisiana affiliated with the MLM. White responded by sending a copy of a letter he had written to Frederick Weyerhaeuser when the white-pine baron had inquired about buying land from an MLM affiliate in Louisiana.[30] It is obvious that White was aware of the country's business climate at the end of the nineteenth century and envisioned himself as a corporate magnate with the ability to seize control of an industry.

---

[27] Galloway, "John Barber White," 71.

[28] Ibid., 73.

[29] J. B. White to J. H. Berkshire, 18 September 1897, folder 1, MLM Records.

[30] J. B. White to Col. O. H. Ingram, 5 June 1901, vol. 9, p. 71, MLM Records.

The exchange enabled White to improve and maintain profits as he found markets for his lumber and disposed of cutover land. In 1897, White reported to his partners in the exchange that on one typical day, the MLM received six orders from the exchange, but seventeen directly from lumberyards throughout the nation. White assured his colleagues that he was working diligently to get all orders routed through the exchange. White also stated that the MLM turned down one to two lumber orders daily in 1897 "because the prices sent us are lower than our [the exchange's] price list."[31] As the primary marketing tool for the yellow pine of many Ozark mills, the exchange enabled White to significantly influence the market. In 1899 alone, he raised timber prices on ten separate occasions.[32] White, the MLM, and the exchange reflected the context of corporate consolidation in search of efficiency that marked the turn of the century. White established himself as the head of a large corporation, allied himself with similar businessmen, and consolidated his hold on the industry through cooperative agreements and price lists.

The exchange offered Missouri's timbermen a wide range of economic opportunities through consolidation. In 1897, George K. Smith, secretary of the exchange, wrote to the affiliated companies, "Gentlemen: The trade papers are after us for advertising." In response to these demands, Smith assessed the costs of such advertisements and determined that they would be "more for the sustaining of the trade papers than for any great good we expect to receive." The economic advantages of the exchange, however, allowed Smith to conclude, "When we do any more advertising, we might do it all together… and thus make the burden lighter on all of us."[33] White and his associates recognized and exploited the benefits of pooling resources.

The Workers

A booming timber industry continued to bring changes to the Ozarks in the last decade of the nineteenth century and the first decade of the twentieth century. As the MLM expanded its operations and continued to build up

[31] J. B. White to members of the Missouri Lumber Exchange, 18 August 1897, folder 1, MLM Records.

[32] Ponder, *Grandin, Hunter, and West Eminence*, 51.

[33] George K. Smith to members of the Missouri Lumber Exchange, 11 August 1897, folder 1, MLM Records.

its labor force, people flooded the region in search of work. In 1900, Carter County's population reached a new high of 6,706, with a population density of more than nine and one half people per square mile.[34]

The increasing demands of lumber production brought people from throughout the Ozarks and across the nation to labor in the mills and woods of the Courtois Hills. In 1900, the MLM had roughly 1,000 employees in Grandin. The company increased its employment in the community to 1,211 by 1903 and to a peak of approximately 1,500 in 1905.[35] The result of this boom in employment and population was that in 1900, the only year with acceptable figures for both, approximately one in every six residents of Carter County was directly employed by the MLM. Even this high number does not account for people working at other mills or selling timber and ties on a contract basis, nor does it include family members. As railroads moved into the Ozarks and industrial production became more intense, population also increased.

The MLM brought foremen, sawyers, managers, and other skilled operatives who had experience in the large-scale timber industry from the Northeast and Great Lakes regions to the Ozarks. Although some of the company's first common laborers came with the company from its homeland of Pennsylvania, the MLM relied primarily on Ozarkers for unskilled labor.[36] The company did not have explicit guidelines concerning hiring, but it did require character references, which it checked thoroughly before employing anyone.[37] By carefully selecting the residents of Grandin, the MLM attempted to create a town devoted to its vision of production and morality in the rugged Courtois Hills.

Timber towns remained a male-dominated landscape, but unmarried women from outside the region constituted an important element of the company's workforce. As stenographers and clerks, these women performed essential duties for the MLM, recording the minutes of meetings and preparing and sending letters and notices. The opportunities for such work attracted

[34] Stevens, *A Homeland and A Hinterland*, 96.

[35] Hill, "History of the Missouri Lumber and Mining Company," 142–43.

[36] Hill, "History of the Missouri Lumber and Mining Company," 149–50; Galloway, "John Barber White," 22; and Loveland, *Two Years in Grandin*, 6, 18.

[37] J. B. White to D. C. Richardson, 27 February 1907, folder 383; C. C. Sheppard to J. B. White, 7 May 1907, folder 438, both in MLM Records; and Ponder, *Grandin, Hunter, and West Eminence*, 60.

women from considerable distances. The MLM's employment of women as clerks and stenographers put the company in the forefront of the feminization of office work as women across the nation began to enter these positions in large numbers in the early 1890s.[38]

As early as 1897, the company appears to have drawn from a national pool of female employees. White wrote to the freight manager of the Union Pacific Railroad to obtain a reduced rate for Miss Maumie Bunker, who wanted to temporarily leave Grandin to visit her family in Silver City, New Mexico.[39] To select qualified female employees, the company often turned to Kansas City business schools.[40] In 1905, White and Sheppard considered four different women to fill a vacant stenographer position before the men hired a woman from Kansas City.[41] As with other vacancies, the MLM filled this position by reviewing letters and recommendations sent to the offices of the Missouri Lumber Exchange in Kansas City.

The influx of women from outside the region and without local family ties to Grandin drastically reshaped the social structure of the region. With company-owned rental homes reserved for families, boardinghouses met the housing needs of single members of the community. The MLM's boardinghouse for unmarried women, which it dubbed "Whitehall" because it was J. B. White's original Grandin home and which town bachelors called "Dear Park," illustrates the influx of unattached women in the community. The company allowed a number of its female employees to reside in the local hotel because the boardinghouse was unable to accommodate the number of women the MLM brought to Grandin.[42]

Boardinghouses were one of the company's key methods of maintaining its vision of morality among its workers in Grandin. When the MLM was looking

---

[38] Fine, *Souls of the Skyscraper*, 26–32.

[39] J. B. White to F. C. Gay, 4 November 1897, folder 1, MLM Records.

[40] Hill, "History of the Missouri Lumber and Mining Company," 150–51. For a discussion of women's entrance into business schools and clerical work, see Fine, *Souls of the Skyscraper*; and Kwolek-Folland, "Gender, Self, and Work."

[41] J. B. White to C. C. Sheppard, 5 September 1905, folder 38, MLM Records.

[42] Grandin *Herald*, 9 November 1905; and Hill, "History of the Missouri Lumber and Mining Company," 154–55. The use of boardinghouses for young, unmarried female employees in Grandin is reminiscent of the well-established "Lowell System." For a brief discussion of the use of boardinghouses in company towns, see Hall, *Like a Family*, esp. 52, 373.

for a man to run one of its men's boardinghouses in 1904, C. C. Sheppard, as the individual responsible for daily operations in Grandin, wrote to the applicants' references to determine not just the character of the potential employees, but of their families as well.[43] Two years later, the manager of the Young Ladies Boarding House, Jennie Ruggles, felt compelled to defend the behavior of her charges and her effectiveness.

> In justice to the young ladies charged with disorder and loud conduct, I must say that I am sure you have been wrongfully informed. It is true they have spent several evenings in the parlor and played and sung, but by no means has it been a nightly occurrence and to my knowledge they have not spent to exceed six evenings in the parlor since the first of September. Occasionally on their return from Church service they have stepped into the parlor for ten or fifteen minutes, but that, as you know, would not be later than nine o'clock.[44]

Ruggles argued that she was aware of the women's actions and that they were beyond reproach. By offsetting any questionable behavior with assertions of religiosity, Ruggles depicted her boarders as observing the morality the company held in high regard for its female and male employees. The MLM expected its laborers to adhere to its idea of acceptable conduct if they planned to remain in Grandin.

Race and ethnicity were also factors the MLM considered in its plans to industrialize the rural South. In her account of the two years she spent as White's personal secretary, Lillian S. Loveland, who was born in Nebraska and moved to Massachusetts after her time in Grandin, discussed the social character of the community. On the issues of race and ethnicity in Grandin, she noted, "There were no colored people, no Italians, or Hungarians." She provided an anecdote to illustrate the racial homogeneity of the community: "One spring when Mrs. White and family spent a month in Grandin, she brought her colored butler along and he attracted a good deal of attention

[43] C. C. Sheppard to Byrd Duncan, 14 April 1904, folder 2185, MLM Records.
[44] Jennie Ruggles to J. B. White, 14 November 1906, folder 261, MLM Records.

as he went about the streets. Some of the children had never before seen a person of his race and looked at him with wondering, half-frightened eyes."[45] Loveland claimed that this information came from W. C. Slagle, a native of Ohio, who gave her tours of the company's holdings. There is no reason to question the veracity of Loveland's account, but she witnessed only a small slice of Grandin's society and for only two years in the late 1890s.

There are indications from the first decade of the twentieth century that black laborers performed valuable services in Carter County. The Grandin *Herald* noted in 1906, "E. L. Blaine returned Monday from Cape Girardeau, where he went to get a bunch of tie loaders from among the colored gents of that place."[46] It is possible that Ozarkers refused to fill the positions; loading railroad ties, which could weigh over 200 pounds, was one of the most physically demanding and unpleasant jobs in the industry (see fig. 9). The MLM's employment of black laborers for tie loading may not have been unique in the region. The *Herald* notes, "The Negroes who are to load the Smalley ties, arrived [in Van Buren] Tuesday. The tie train is expected Wednesday."[47] The

Figure 9: "Black Railroad Crew" (folder 2, MLM Company Photographs, 1906–1916, WHMC–Columbia).

[45] Loveland, *Two Years in Grandin*, 18.
[46] Grandin *Herald*, 4 January 1906.
[47] Grandin *Herald*, 22 November 1906.

Smalley Tie and Timber Company brought black men to Van Buren to complete a necessary task, but did not welcome the laborers to the community for an extended period. There is only one other mention of black laborers in the Grandin *Herald*, also as tie loaders. Because tie loading was one of the least desirable jobs available, the MLM and other companies may have turned to importing black men as laborers despite industrialists' qualms about upsetting white workers.[48]

In a series of letters to fellow mill owners, White revealed his opinions on the role of black labor in the southern timber industry. He first wrote to W. W. Warren in Louisiana and declared that the MLM and its affiliates could not allow local whites to prevent the timber industry from hiring blacks.[49] A letter to another timberman was more revealing. White stated, "I understand that the natives seem determined to have no Negro work at our mill."[50] White does not make it clear which mills he is discussing until he offers Homer Vaughn of Texarkana, Texas, the role of protecting and supervising the company's black labor in Louisiana.[51] The MLM apparently made an effort to prevent black men from living in Grandin; however, when black labor provided the most efficient solution to a problem, such as a labor shortage in Louisiana, White made every effort to exploit what he probably saw as a practical answer.

Control of Infrastructure and Education

Ownership of all housing and infrastructure in Grandin provided the MLM another means of maintaining economic and social control. In 1906, a woman wrote C. C. Sheppard asking for work in the company offices. When Sheppard asked White for advice on the application the general manager replied, "I think you had better tell her that houses are scarce.... But you might say to her in another year about one-third of our houses will be empty, as we expect to stop running nights."[52] This episode suggests several things: Grandin was open

---

[48] For a discussion of black laborers' roles in the construction and maintenance of the nation's railroad system, see Arnesen, *Brotherhoods of Color*. For a treatment of black workers' success in entering the mining industry, see Trotter, *Coal, Class, and Color*.

[49] J. B. White to W. W. Warren, 2 October 1899, vol. 3. pp. 31–32; and J. B. White to W. W. Warren, 3 October 1899, vol. 3, pp. 40–41, both letters in MLM Records.

[50] J. B. White to C. W. Fisher, 5 October 1899, vol. 3, p. 54, MLM Records.

[51] J. B. White to Homer Vaughn, 6 October 1899, vol. 3, p. 64, MLM Records.

[52] J. B. White to C. C. Sheppard, 31 January 1906, folder 83, MLM Records.

to women seeking jobs, the MLM restricted residence in Grandin to employ-ees, the company was experiencing a downturn in productivity, and White maintained control at a detailed level even though Sheppard handled most of the local managerial duties. This is also a good illustration of the relationship between White and Sheppard, a relationship White mentioned more than once as an example of his beneficence. When the MLM moved to the Ozarks, White had hired C. C. Sheppard and his three orphaned siblings, all of whom worked their way into positions of responsibility.[53] Despite White's assertions, this was not a representative example of corporate and local relations.

The company also used its ownership of all housing in Grandin for social assistance. The MLM generally assisted women who lost husbands at work by providing a small payment, subsidizing their rent for up to two years, and occasionally providing the widows with a sewing machine.[54] In some cases the MLM allowed widows to remain in the community for a longer period, even when they remained unemployed and had difficulty caring for their families. In 1907 the company repaired a Mrs. Brooks's cistern, including new troughs and a new gravel and charcoal filter because, as White said, "I know that our Company will feel better to finish it up as she has no money."[55] It is uncer-tain why the company moved away from its emphasis on profits in these in-stances. Did the MLM intend to gain the goodwill of Grandin's residents by helping needy widows? On the other hand, this may have been part of a larger pattern of paternalism, in which the MLM demonstrated some responsibility for people in Grandin whom it considered dependents.

Modern amenities such as sidewalks and telephones came to Grandin when the MLM decided the benefits of such developments outweighed the costs. To facilitate business, the company constructed a sidewalk through the center of town. As the *Herald* noted, "That new sidewalk along Main Street

[53] J. B. White to R. J. Thompson, 23 February 1906, folder 107, MLM Records. To compare the actions of the MLM to the development of other company towns during the late nineteenth and early twentieth centuries, see Hall, *Like a Family*; and Trotter, *Coal, Class, and Color*.

[54] J. B White to Sarah Carmody, 11 December 1889, folder 6726; J. B. White to Mrs. Thomas Miner, 11 October 1890, folder 6727; and J. B. White to Mrs. Gunnett, 13 March 1891, folder 6728, all in MLM Records.

[55] J. B. White to C. C. Sheppard, 12 October 1907, folder 623, MLM Records. This was probably Emeline Brooks, a native of Tennessee noted in the census of 1900 as being a widow in Carter Township, Carter County, Missouri.

is the real thing and is duly appreciated by everyone."[56] The next summer, 1907, local residents urged the company to construct more sidewalks to make life in town more bearable. White explained, "As I have said many times, our Company is not building sidewalks to the different houses on the different streets in Grandin, but wherever we have built a walk it is a duty to keep it up, but we do not wish to add to our burdens nor our liabilities."[57] The company wanted to bring its version of civilization and modernity to the Ozarks, in the form of cleanliness and productivity, but not at the cost of profits. Local people sought and accepted those elements of the company's vision for the town that they believed would improve their lives without reducing their connections to their past.

The MLM brought the telephone to Grandin because, much like sidewalks, it made business more efficient. The company created a private telephone line to link Grandin with Van Buren and Centerville, the seat of Reynolds County, but when locals asked permission to install telephones in their homes, White resisted.[58] The MLM's policy was that residents could make no alterations to their homes without explicit approval. White finally relented and told George Willett (a local real estate agent, notary public, and a commissioner of the Grandin State Bank, who frequently spoke on behalf of the community's workers) that it was acceptable as long as the workers would assume all charges involved with the installation and operation of the telephones. The company's general manager demanded, "We want it perfectly understood that there is to be no liability on the part of the Mo. Lumber & Mining Co."[59] After residents made the changes, the infrastructure became another element the company could use to draw skilled workers to Grandin. The MLM speeded the pace of modernization in the Ozarks, but only when it proved profitable.

The company recognized education as an ideal medium through which it could inculcate its employees with its values. During the late nineteenth and early twentieth century, William Torrey Harris led a national movement to reform the nation's educational system. After beginning as an educator within

[56] Grandin *Herald*, 16 August 1906.

[57] J. B. White to C. C. Sheppard, 30 July 1907, folder 528, MLM Records.

[58] Hill, "History of the Missouri Lumber and Mining Company," 240.

[59] J. B. White to George Willett, 4 May 1907, folder 434, MLM Records.

the St. Louis public school system, he moved on to become the U.S. commissioner of education. Harris tried to shape education so it could indoctrinate children into an industrialized America and to ensure that future generations would have the skills necessary to become productive members of society.[60] A note from the John L. Boland Book & Stationery Company of St. Louis provides some insight into the MLM's schools. Boland writes to inform the MLM that he is having trouble obtaining the copy of Phillip's & Fisher's *Plane Geometry*, fourteen copies of *Evangeline*, and twenty copies of Hawthorne's *Three Golden Apples* that the timbermen had ordered.[61] This reading list is a wonderful illustration of the company's efforts to present Grandin's youth with a combination of scientific knowledge, pastoral idealism, and Victorian morality. There is no conclusive evidence that these books were intended for the school, but it seems likely.

The company served as the patron of Grandin's school, constructing the building (fig. 10), accepting the costs of maintenance, and working to form

Figure 10: "School House, 1907" (folder 1, p. 6a, MLM Company Photographs, 1906–1916, WHMC–Columbia).

---

[60] Thelen, *Paths of Resistance*, 108–10.

[61] John L. Boland to Missouri Lumber & Mining Company, 14 September 1904, folder 2099, MLM Records.

strong relationships with the students. According to Hill, "The superintendent of the mills was usually president of the school board, and the board generally consulted the general manager before employing teachers or before adopting any important school measure." White even employed two of his children as teachers to ensure that the community's youth received what he considered an appropriate education.[62] The company also inserted itself into the lives of students by providing gifts to all high school graduates at least from 1904 to 1907.[63] This benevolence aided the MLM in its efforts to identify individuals who had valuable skills and an interest in the timber industry.

Leonard Hawn's relationship with the MLM illustrates the connection between the company and the school. Hawn, both of whose parents were born in Missouri, applied for work as the company was decreasing its employment in response to poor economic conditions in the timber industry in 1907. Sheppard informed White that "Leonard Hawn's father, of course, expects to leave us when we get through in Carter and Reynolds Counties." Sheppard then explained, "Leonard having graduated here from the public school thinks he would like to take this work and stay here with a view of learning as much as he can about the business."[64] This instance recalls Thelen's argument that people and institutions that encouraged a cultural shift to align society more closely with industry understood the utility of education for changing the beliefs of traditional Missourians.[65] The ability to shape the minds of young Ozarkers, a goal of both the MLM and later the U.S. Forest Service and the Missouri Department of Conservation, was by no means unique. In a similar environment, reformers in Appalachia were undertaking social engineering through the introduction of education to people who had previously missed the opportunity.[66]

Women felt the effects of education at least as deeply as men in Grandin. Women played a significant role in the educational system as students and

[62] Hill, "History of the Missouri Lumber and Mining Company," 246–47.

[63] J. B. White to C. C. Sheppard, 13 June 1905, folder 29; C. C. Sheppard to J. B. White, 25 May 1906, folder 177; and J. B. White to C. C. Sheppard, 16 May 1907, folder 446, all letters in MLM Records.

[64] C. C. Sheppard to J. B. White, 30 May 1907, folder 471, MLM Records.

[65] Thelen, *Paths of Resistance*, 108–16.

[66] Williams, *Appalachia*, 202.

teachers. Girls comprised the entire graduating class from the high school in 1906; four boys and four girls graduated in 1907.[67] Many Ozark schools also had women as teachers, as demonstrated in the annual teachers' meeting for Carter County in 1905, when women made up the vast majority of the twenty-six attendees.[68] The MLM's papers demonstrate that most of these female teachers came from outside the region and only stayed in Grandin temporarily. The women who came to the Ozark timber towns from other areas made valuable contributions to the intellectual, social, and religious development of their new communities.

Control of Leisure Time and Amenities

When it established company towns and logging camps, the MLM designed strategies to shape the social attitudes of a labor force largely unaccustomed to industry. The company utilized several strategies, such as attempting to control leisure activities and to funnel all commerce through company stores to meet corporate goals of productivity. In addition to combating drunkenness (although White did order alcohol for himself and his guests), gambling, and disturbing the peace, the MLM also maintained a library, an athletic and band association, and a Baptist, a Congregationalist, and a Methodist (and occasionally a Catholic and an Episcopalian) church.[69] The company provided these amenities to encourage their employees to accept a middle-class vision of morality and a culture of productivity in the context of the market economy.

The Grandin Reading Room and Library Association organized in 1899 "to promote the intellectual growth of the community by supplying interesting reading matter and by such other means as may come within the province of a Library Association."[70] In addition to supporting the intellectual and

---

[67] C. C. Sheppard to J. B. White, 25 May 1906, folder 177; and J. B. White to C. C. Sheppard, 16 May 1907, folder 446, both letters in MLM Records.

[68] Grandin *Herald*, 19 October 1905.

[69] C. C. Sheppard to R. W. Cook, [31 August 1906?], folder 224; J. B. White to William Warner, 29 January 1906, folder 80; and C. C. Sheppard to J. B. White, 19 June 1906, folder 189, all items in MLM Records.

[70] "Constitution and By-Laws of the Grandin Reading-Room and Library Association," 4 March 1899, folder 6910; "Grandin Reading Room and Library Association," no date, folder 6910; and "Recommendation of Board of Trustees of Library Association," no date, folder 6913, all items in MLM Records.

social development of Grandin, the library provided educated women with a prominent position in the cultural life of the community. Both women and men held the offices of chairman and secretary, while a Miss Coon and a Miss Smith served as the association's librarians throughout the institution's recorded history.[71] White considered the library important enough that he set up an insurance policy in 1905 to cover the association's building, furniture, and books.[72] The existence and actions of the library demonstrate the MLM's efforts to end the cultural isolation of the Courtois Hills residents and provide opportunities for educated men and women who embraced the new society emerging in the company town.

Leisure time offered employees an opportunity to escape the mills and offices of Grandin and attempt to maintain important traditions. In reality, however many leisure activities remained strongly tied to the MLM. Local residents spent their free time participating in social associations, playing sports, hunting, gambling, and going to church. Each of these activities contributed significantly to the development of the community. Residents of Grandin and the surrounding hills enthusiastically participated in social organizations. Each week the *Herald* listed the associations in the community and detailed their meetings and activities. The paper kept track of at least eight associations, including the Knights of Pythias, Knights of the Maccabees, Modern Day Woodmen of America, Odd Fellows, Royal Neighbors of America, Rebeccahs, Court of Honor, and Ladies of the Maccabees. These associations included gender-specific as well as mixed groups.[73] Men and women found the opportunities to participate in company-approved recreation, a valuable part of community life.

Another association the company assisted was the Knights of King Arthur (K.O.K.A.). The MLM recognized the knights as an institution capable of helping the company maintain a manageable and productive labor force in Grandin. In a letter to Marion Edward Rhodes, a Republican from Potosi, Missouri, who served in the U.S. House of Representatives from 1905 to 1906 and again from 1919 to 1921, White identified a key aspect of the

[71] "Grandin Reading Room and Library Association," no date, folder 6911, MLM Records.

[72] Receipt for insurance premium, signed by J. B. White, 18 April 1905, folder 20, MLM Records.

[73] Grandin *Herald*, 2 November 1905.

company's management strategy: "We have been trying to make good men out of the boys. We have three churches and as good a school as there is in southeast Missouri, a public library, a gymnasium and a lot of workers who are trying to make good boys and good men."[74] W. R. Bosard, then deacon of the Congregational Church, informed White, "Two of the tobacco-using boys of the town were going to, or had quit using tobacco so that they can join the K.O.K.A."[75] The knights furthered the MLM's efforts to promote a healthy and productive workforce. White informed Sheppard, "If good can be done by getting the young men into the K.O.K.A. to work, and if he [Bosard] can get in some more boys and establish an industrial department, the Grandins offer to give the money to buy the tools; our Company will pay toward that institution $15.00 a month and will furnish the lumber for the shop."[76] The MLM may not have had long-term plans for the town, but it did work to mold the population into a useful resource.[77]

The MLM seems to have recognized the importance of social associations as a means of controlling the leisure time of its employees. These associations, generally led by company officials, helped the MLM keep the town's residents happy and moving towards modernity. The Grandin Athletic and Band Association is a good example of an association closely tied to the company (fig. 11). George Willett, proprietor of the Southwest Land and Orchard Company of Grandin and a founding member of the association, thanked White for providing the site and lumber, then added, "We are putting on at our own expense an addition ... for two dressing rooms, one for ladies & one for gentlemen, with a room for shower bath between. We have ordered our shower bath fixtures feeling quite confident that your belief in cleanliness being next to godliness would justify you in allowing us to use the water from the company pipes."[78] Willett knew this appeal to the MLM's beneficence and its desire for a healthy and clean community would bolster his case to gain additional support for the association. White assented to the association's free use of MLM utilities and continued to support its activities.

[74] J. B. White to M. E. Rhodes, 23 February 1906, folder 107, MLM Records.

[75] W. R. Bosard to J. B. White, 11 February 1907, folder 362, MLM Records.

[76] J. B. White to C. C. Sheppard, 1 August 1907, folder 530, MLM Records.

[77] For a discussion of similar issues, see Rosenzweig, *Eight Hours for What We Will.*

[78] George Willett to J. B. White, 5 April 1905, folder 18, MLM Records.

Figure 11: "Grandin Athletic & Band Association Building" (folder 2, p. a, MLM Company Photographs, 1906–1916, WHMC–Columbia).

As an institution upholding and promoting morality and healthfulness, the Athletic and Band Association was able to maintain a strong relationship with the MLM.

The company's largess also benefited other organizations when the Athletic and Band Association made its hall available to other groups such as the Junior Boys' Club, Boys' Military Organization, Grandin Hoo Hoo Band, Young Ladies' Club, Young Men's Club, Boys' Club, Junior Girls' Club, and the Girls' Club.[79] The Athletic and Band Association was probably the most active social institution in the community. In 1906, the association had a membership of seventy-nine individuals, including eighteen unmarried and

---

[79] George Willett to J. B. White, 8 April 1905, folder 18; J. B. White to George Willett, 7 April 1905, folder 18; and Minutes of the Grandin Athletic and Band Association, 21 March 1906, folder 6909, all items in MLM Records.

nine married women.[80] Whether or not it did so consciously, the associa-tion provided the MLM with tools to control workers' activities (including organized baseball games and band recitals) when they were not in the mills, logging camps, or offices. Timber companies exploited every means available to steer employees' minds and actions in acceptable directions.

Sporting activities were an important part of the social life of Grandin's residents. The Grandin Athletic and Band Association had a key role in en-couraging participation in leisure activities that community reformers ac-cepted wholeheartedly. The association opened its gymnasium to Grandin's residents with several restrictions: "Card playing in or about the gymnasium building at any time, the use of tobacco in any form, the use of intoxicants or being in an intoxicated condition, bad language and spitting on the floor will not be tolerated."[81] The association offered opportunities to locals, but only if the participants accepted the ideals of Victorian propriety espoused by the company.

This relationship was also evident when the association convinced the MLM to help it open a skating rink. This is significant partly because the as-sociation's plan met with condemnation from the ministers of the Congrega-tional, Methodist, and Baptist churches. The MLM and the town's churches generally agreed on policies. In the case of the skating rink, however, C. C. Sheppard, who was president of the association and the local manager of the MLM, may have had the last say.[82] The association provided leisure opportu-nities for locals, while it combated those behaviors the company considered unacceptable.

Sports, particularly baseball, were an important element of many Ozark communities. Maintaining teams was one way the MLM directed men's lei-sure activities. In *Ozark Baptizings, Hangings, and Other Diversions* (1984), Robert Gilmore discussed the particular appeal of baseball for Ozarkers. Baseball provided hill folk an opportunity to compete against other towns

---

[80] Membership roll, Grandin Athletic and Band Association, 1 October 1906, folder 6909, MLM Records.

[81] By Laws Governing the Use of the G. A. B. Gymnasium, Department of Members, no date, folder 6909, MLM Records.

[82] Minutes of the Grandin Athletic and Band Association, 4 December 1906, folder 6909, MLM Records.

throughout the region.[83] Grandin supported at least two baseball teams and the *Herald* regularly reported on the play of teams and individuals in numerous letters and editorials for weeks before and after games. Grandin residents also created an all-star team from their regular squads to compete against neighboring communities in matches covered by the *Herald*.[84]

Religion was another aspect of the social life in Grandin where the company attempted to direct the transition to a society based on production, efficiency, and middle-class morality. While operating its mills in the community, the MLM built and maintained at least three churches and paid the salaries of their ministers.[85] It is uncertain how much control White had over what went on in the churches, but the ministers would undoubtedly have had at least some loyalty to the source of their salaries. With White as a member, W. C. Slagle, proprietor of the company store, as an occasional deacon, and the Knights of King Arthur as a community outreach program, the Congregational Church (fig. 12) was especially well connected to the company,[86] and the church building presents a stunning example of Victorian architecture to complement the morality the company upheld. It is also significant that the Congregational Church was the only place of worship of which a photograph was preserved in the MLM's records. Whether the company tried to influence religious doctrine or not, churches could encourage a middle-class morality and the Protestant work ethic.

The company claimed to support any faith whose representatives found an interested congregation in the community. At various times, Grandin was home to Episcopalian and Catholic congregations whose priests traveled between churches throughout the Ozarks, but received salaries from the MLM equal to those of resident religious leaders.[87] As early as 1897, White made it a policy "to give each one of the Sunday Schools $15.00" for Christmas. In that year, he noted that he knew of two Sunday schools in the community, but

[83] Gilmore, *Ozark Baptizings, Hangings, and Other Diversions*, 142–46.

[84] Grandin *Herald*, 19 July 1906; 6 September 1906.

[85] J. B. White to C. C. Sheppard, 13 May 1905, folder 24; and J. B. White to Wm. Warner, 29 January 1905, folder 80, both letters in MLM Records.

[86] R. Bosard to J. B. White, 11 February 1907, folder 362; and J. B. White to C. C. Sheppard, 1 August 1907, folder 530, both letters in MLM Records.

[87] F. W. Wright to J. B. White, 9 January 1907, folder 309; and F. W. Wright to J. B. White, 10 January 1907, folder 311, both letters in MLM Records.

Figure 12: "Congregational Church" (folder 1, p. 7, MLM Company Photographs, 1906–1916, WHMC–Columbia).

if there were three he would contribute equally to each institution.[88] White did not mention which churches sponsored the Sunday schools, but it is safe to assume that the Congregational Church was one of them. By funding the Knights of King Arthur and Sunday schools, and by attending services, the MLM and its officers took advantage of the socializing elements of religion to create and maintain a manageable labor force that conformed to its ideas of propriety.

Women who wished to demonstrate leadership in the MLM's communities were able to capitalize on the importance of religious institutions in the company's efforts at social organization. Women frequently served as the carriers of information and money between the MLM and churches. F. W. Wright, the company's chief cashier, reported to White, "Miss Maguire has just handed me your letter of Dec. 29th, and as instructed therein, I have given her $10.00 for a Christmas present to Father Smyth, the Catholic priest,

[88] J. B. White to W. C. Slagle, 23 December 1897, vol. 1, p. 76, MLM Records.

who has been officiating here of late."[89] In another instance, White returned a letter to Sheppard from Mrs. Ora Kelley, a Missouri native, with the comment that "she appears to be Secretary of the Church Society, and I note they want to build a church at Hunter [about five miles north of Grandin]. You will recollect that I gave them a Mo. Lumber & Mining Company check, and I told them that we would give them a lot. My first promise was to give them a lot in case they built a schoolhouse."[90] Despite the misunderstanding over the purpose of the MLM's support, it is significant that Mrs. Kelley served as the intermediary between the company and the residents of Hunter. The episode also demonstrates White's commitment to both education and religion. Throughout the nation, women often turned to opportunities supported by religious institutions to take a greater role in public life.[91]

At the turn of the century, organized religion provided company employees with an opportunity for socializing. Women worked through the community's religious institutions to provide their neighbors with wholesome entertainment. Each church created distinct social events and assumed a unique role in Grandin's social life. The ladies' aid society of the Congregational Church organized bazaars to support the church and its activities. The Methodist Church's ladies' aid society conducted regular sewing club meetings, ice cream socials, and bazaars, while the women of the Baptist Church primarily restricted their efforts to pie suppers.[92]

Pie suppers provide historians a unique look into the culture of the Ozarks. In *Ozark Baptizings, Hangings, and Other Diversions*, Gilmore describes how at first glance the pie supper was a simple fund-raiser where women and girls of the community baked pies and brought them to the auction site to draw bids from the community's men. The pie supper, however, was a much more complex social event. In addition to the pie, the high bidder won the privilege of a date with the pastry's maker, whose identity was kept secret until after the bidding. Pie suppers offered young women and men an opportunity to gather

[89] F. W. Wright to J. B. White, 2 January 1907, folder 297, MLM Records.

[90] J. B. White to C. C. Sheppard, 11 January 1907, folder 315, MLM Records.

[91] Blair, *Clubwoman as Feminist*.; and Scott, *Natural Allies*. Both mention the importance of religious institutions as a basis for women's organizations.

[92] Grandin *Herald*, 19 October 1905, 16 November 1905, and 22 February 1906. These are the most detailed of several reports on each faith's activities.

and interact in a socially accepted setting under the oversight of the community.[93] The documentation surrounding church-sponsored pie suppers in Grandin does not elaborate on the fund-raisers. It seems likely, however, that the residents of the MLM town followed the traditions of other Ozarkers.

Religion could also demonstrate the emerging diversity in the region. Although individuals of German heritage have probably had more impact on Missouri than any other ethnic group, they played a minor role in the Ozarks. Gerlach explained that because of their cultural propensities to establish communities where they could create large and profitable farms, few Germans settled in the Courtois Hills. The rugged topography and poor soils of the interior Ozarks made productive farming difficult, which led to a small German population in the region.[94] Germans may not have been common in the region, but they were present. In 1905, a couple born in Germany had their child christened at Grandin's Congregational Church. The minister performed the service in both German and English.[95] Because this christening occurred at the Congregational Church, it encourages a great deal of speculation. Could the company have seen Germans as a potential source of skilled labor and attempted to create a friendly environment in Grandin? This christening may also have been an isolated incident where a skilled worker from the company's homeland of Pennsylvania desired special accommodations. Regardless of the specifics of the event, it is an example of the MLM's willingness to provide services to its valuable workers who chose to patronize such approved institutions as the Congregational Church.

Maintaining Productivity

In addition to keeping its workers occupied with acceptable pursuits in their leisure time, the company recognized the importance of keeping laborers healthy and productive when in its forests, mills, and offices. To accomplish this, the company began to keep a small staff of doctors and to maintain a hospital for employees and their families as early as 1890.[96] Each month, the

---

[93] Gilmore, *Ozark Baptizings, Hangings, and Other Diversions*, 103–10.

[94] Gerlach, *Immigrants in the Ozarks*, 28–30, 41–43.

[95] Grandin *Herald*, 19 October 1905.

[96] Missouri Lumber and Mining Company account book, 1891–1892, vol. 84, p. 2, MLM Records.

company collected seventy-five cents from single men and a dollar twenty-five from family men to support the hospital association. This association accepted responsibility for supplying the hospital and paying the doctors. Sheppard claimed that the MLM merely collected for and directed the association, which the residents of Grandin had created voluntarily.[97] With such a structure for the hospital association, the MLM remained free of the expense and trivial details of oversight while holding the purse strings of health care for its workers.

Following company ideals of proper behavior proved valuable when employees suffered injuries on the job. The MLM generally provided injured employees with assistance when they were deemed worthy. In 1906, Sheppard relayed an account of C. M. Randolph's injury to White: "He was running the slasher and a small piece of lumber; not more than 1" square was thrown by one of the trimmer saws and struck him just above the eye, which was quite painful and it seemed as if his eye might be seriously injured at first; but he has almost entirely recovered and will return to work Monday, October 15th." Sheppard then stated, "We note your instructions that he is in need and worthy we should help him to the extent of allowing his house rent or furnishing him provisions from our store."[98] The MLM assisted individuals who subscribed to its vision of a productive workforce, but refused to support workers who demanded help. Hill notes that "Although the corporation was occasionally sued, there is no record of an employee or his family ever winning damages."[99]

The MLM often dealt with death and injury to its railroad workers, especially brakemen and top loaders who occasionally fell between cars in the course of their duties. These men rarely escaped with their lives. The report of the MLM's Texas-born chief physician, Dr. Alexander Johnston, on the injury of Phillip Clark in 1891 is one of the most illustrative of many examples. When Clark attempted to grab a brake lever he fell between two moving railroad cars:

[97] C. C. Sheppard to R. W. Cook, 1 September 1906, folder 224, MLM Records.

[98] C. C. Sheppard to J. B. White, 13 October 1906, folder 249, MLM Records.

[99] Hill, "History of the Missouri Lumber and Mining Company," 170–73.

The wheel caught the heel of his right foot. Crushing it, then dragging the leg and ankle under it, and in turn crushing and mangling it also, following it up the thigh it severed, lacerated & contused the muscles, veins, arteries, nerves etc, including the femoral artery and vein and anterior crucial nerves into an almost disorganized mass, breaking the large bone of the thigh (femur) in twain about 4 inches above the knee joints, then stripping the muscles from the upper end of the fractured bone, lacerating and contusing the bone and its covering (the periosteum) to an extent of six inches from the fracture—The loss of blood, and the shock to the nervous system was very great.

Clark died about a week after the injury, despite the doctors' best efforts.[100] This episode received a more detailed description than most, but it was not uncommon. In the company's papers, the frequency of serious accidents is revealed by the seven folders containing nothing other than the most dramatic injury reports.[101] That Clark's accident does not appear in any other correspondence or in the Van Buren *Current Local*, the primary newspaper in the area at the time, suggests a certain amount of acceptance among Ozarkers and the MLM of such accidents as a normal part of life in a timber town.

The testimony of an employee named Allen Waite concerning the 1894 death of Charles Kitchell, a brakeman, provides another example. Waite stated that Kitchell's "foot slipped through the step and his hold gave way on the ladder." Waite then adds detail to his testimony by explaining that the cars dragged Kitchell "fully forty feet" and claims, "I saw him after he had fallen when cars were dragging him."[102] In the 1890s alone, the MLM lost at least fifteen men to railroad accidents. Brakemen on the MLM's tramlines suffered the most frequent and serious injuries. Discussing one of his patients, Dr. Johnston stated, "He was a railroad brakeman by occupation and had met

---

[100] Alexander Johnston, Notarized report of accident and treatment, 10 January 1891, folder 6729, MLM Records.

[101] Folders 6726 through 6733, MLM Records, contain accident reports and related depositions. Volume 148, 27 March 1893 to 17 April 1897, MLM Records, is a record of MLM doctors' activities between 1893 and 1897; it includes descriptions of common injuries and sicknesses, along with treatments administered.

[102] Testimony of Allen Waite before J. P. Riley, 29 December 1894, folder 6733, MLM Records.

with many accidents during that service."[103] This concise statement summed up the patient's medical history and dismissed the uniqueness of the injury that led to his death. Despite the MLM's attempts to keep its employees working productively, serious injury was a regular part of laborers' lives. The company recognized this danger, but also knew railroads were essential to success in the Missouri timber industry.

Timber Harvest and Its Environmental Consequences

During the boom years of Missouri's timber industry, corporations employed large numbers of men to remove the most valuable trees from the forests. Years of woodland burning and free-range grazing had effectively eliminated undergrowth that would have been in the logger's way, but clear-cutting was neither technologically feasible nor economically practical. Rather than clear its land of all standing timber, the MLM generally instructed its loggers to cut no tree smaller than fourteen inches in diameter (see fig. 13).[104] This practice was a response to the technological limitations loggers faced in the early twentieth century as well as industrialists' attitude that forests were inexhaustible. Dependent on men with axes and crosscut saws to fell trees and teamsters with mules and chains to drag logs up poles and load them onto railroad cars for transport to the mills, it was not an economical use of labor to cut smaller timber (see fig. 14). Because logging at the time was very labor intensive, the company only cut those trees offering obvious profit.

The forests of the Ozarks faced many problems at the turn of the century. Large mills harvested only the most valuable trees, but their loggers often damaged smaller trees in the process. Tom Martin recalled the woods of Shannon and Dent Counties during his youth (the early twentieth century): "When I was a kid there was virgin timber here, lots of big pine, oak, and they cut this and skidded it with mules."[105] Farmers, however, often posed a more serious threat as they cleared all of the forestland along river bottoms to plant crops, then burned what remained and ranged livestock on the surrounding

---

[103] Statement of Alexander Johnston, 8 September 1891, folder 6729, MLM Records.

[104] D. J. Stack, "Shortleaf Pine," Columbia *Daily Tribune*, 11 May 1978, Countryside section, p. 17.

[105] Tom Martin and Minnie Martin, interview by Alexander Primm, 19–20 May 1992.

Figure 13: "Men Cutting Trees" (folder 1, p. 17a, MLM Company Photographs, 1906–1916, WHMC–Columbia).

Figure 14: "Three Crews Loading Railroad Cars with Logs" (folder 1, p. 7, MLM Company Photographs, 1906–1916, WHMC–Columbia).

hills.[106] The combination of harvesting timber, burning underbrush for live-stock, and clearing trees for agriculture left the region's forests dramatically impoverished.

As the valuable pine from the Ozark woodlands disappeared, Missouri's timber industry passed its peak and struggled to remain profitable. In 1897, Carter County exported 26,811,000 board feet of lumber. By 1901, produc-tion had risen to 65,946,349 board feet of softwood lumber and 36,000 board feet of hardwood lumber. This proved to be the mill's peak year in Grandin. Though it never reached full capacity, the mill's ability to produce 75 million board feet of lumber per year marked the Grandin facility as the world's largest lumber mill in 1900 and 1901.[107] Lumber output fell to only 36,905,000 board feet of pine lumber and 180,000 feet of hardwood lumber for Carter County in 1904.[108] State lumber production roughly paralleled the Grandin mill during the timber boom. In 1899, Missouri's timber industry produced 715,968,000 board feet of lumber, but declined rapidly thereafter (see fig. 15).[109] After 1900, the MLM and Missouri faced a rapidly declining timber industry. Other than a temporary spike during World War II, Missouri's timber industry would not witness sustained recovery until the 1960s.

One explanation for the industry's troubles as the twentieth century dawned was overuse of the region's forests. In 1897, the Missouri Bureau of Labor Statistics and Inspection reported that the hillsides of Carter County were "covered with heavy pine, oak and walnut forests."[110] Two years later, the same agency again inspected Carter County and reported, "About 80 percent of the land is being cultivated. A small acreage is yet in timber, con-sisting of several varieties of oak, hickory, elm, walnut, ash, maple, cherry, and cottonwood."[111] The pine was gone, the timber scattered, and residents were returning to farming. This clearly demonstrates the rapid progress of the

[106] Westveld, *Applied Silviculture in the United States*, 202–4.

[107] Hill, "History of the Missouri Lumber and Mining Company," 78.

[108] Missouri Bureau of Labor Statistics, *Annual Report, 1897*, 85; Mo. Bureau of Labor Statistics, *Annual Report, 1901*, 170; and Mo. Bureau of Labor Statistics, *Annual Report, 1904*, 25. The report for 1897 did not distinguish between softwood and hardwood production.

[109] Von Schrenk, "Report of the Missouri Forestry Commission," sect. 48, p. 6.

[110] Mo. Bureau of Labor Statistics, *Annual Report, 1897*, 42.

[111] Mo. Bureau of Labor Statistics, *Annual Report, 1899*, 166.

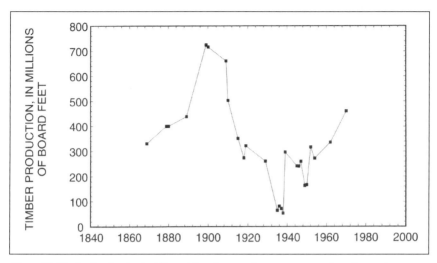

Figure 15: Timber Production in Missouri (Jacobson and Primm, *Historical Land-Use Changes and Potential Effects on Stream Disturbance in the Ozark Plateaus, Missouri*. U.S. Geological Survey Water-Supply Paper 2484, 1997, p. 24).

industry through a single county, a pattern that was mirrored throughout the surrounding countryside.

Preparing for the End

After decimating the state's forests, many large timber operations copied the behavior of their counterparts throughout the nation and simply migrated to more forested areas (i.e., the South and the Northwest), leaving Missouri with a large amount of cutover land in the Ozarks. Missouri's timber companies felt little need to pursue conservation in the first decade of the twentieth century, as demonstrated by the results of the National Conservation Commission's questionnaires to timber companies regarding forestry practices in 1907. Only nine timber operations in Missouri returned the form and none of those firms practiced any fire protection—only one considered forestry practical. In addition, Missouri's timber companies combined to hold only 612 acres of cutover land that they planned to manage for future harvest.[112] Missouri's timbermen had not yet begun to consider forest management profitable.

---

[112] Chapman, "Methods Which Should Be Adopted by Private Owners," 718.

Rather than actively work towards the conservation of its lands, the Missouri Lumber and Land Exchange decided to exploit the forests and then sell off the vast areas of cutover land. The company followed the actions of the declining timber operations of the Great Lakes region by marketing cutover lands as ideal for agriculture and available at low prices.[113] As early as 1898, White wrote on behalf of the exchange to J. E. Defenbaugh, editor of the trade journal *The Timberman*, to include the following text in a lengthy advertisement addressing the company's objectives and business activities:

> The Missouri Lumber & Land Exchange Co. has for sale 65,000 acres of the finest fruit land in the state, being 15,000 acres in Shannon County, 10,000 acres in Oregon County, 30,000 acres in Carter County, and 10,000 acres in Ripley County. These lands are good for agricultural purposes as well as for fruit and will raise corn and wheat and make good homes for thousands, and there will be added from the cutover lands of these three companies, fully 20,000 acres each year. Special inducements will be offered to colonies.[114]

Only nine years after beginning production in Grandin, White was already thinking about ways to liquidate unwanted lands. But despite its efforts, the MLM continued to struggle in its attempts to find willing buyers for its cutover lands.

This effort to dispose of unwanted lands occupied a great deal of the time of various MLM officials. Only one year after running his advertisement for fruit land in an assortment of magazines, White entertained the idea of a colonization scheme: "Mr. Homer Reed of this city [Kansas City] has come to me with a proposition to sell our cutover lands. He wants an option on 50,000 acres for $50,000; wants us to set apart 10,000 acres as an experiment. He has a party who colonized a large section of land in Georgia who has had a party examine our lands in Carter County."[115] White recommended the

---

[113] Gough, *Farming the Cutover*, 18–47.

[114] J. B. White to J. E. Defenbaugh, 27 May 1898, folder 1a, MLM Records.

[115] J. B. White to L. L. Hunter, 28 September 1899, vol. 3, pp. 13–14, MLM Records.

proposal to the MLM's board of directors, but there is no indication that they carried through on it. This is not the only case of such settlement schemes. In 1906, George Willett "settled several Hungarian families, who have recently come from the Old Country, on land in the Hungarian settlement, east of Grandin."[116] Despite continuous and concerted efforts, the MLM would still be struggling to dispose of unwanted land well into the 1930s.

Cutover presented the MLM with a significant problem as the state continued to tax the lands and buyers were often nonexistent. By the early years of the twentieth century, White had already begun trying to donate cutover land to the federal government. He may have been motivated in part by his conservationist leanings, but White certainly considered this effort a good business decision. On Valentine's Day 1905, White informed Sheppard, "I want to know what the tract of land would look like if we would deed all of our land back to the United States; hence I would like to know what we have in cutover and uncut lands as shown on the map. There is no hurry, but I want it put in shape so I can send it to a party in Washington." Less than two weeks later, White wrote Sheppard commenting on an article that mentioned the MLM's efforts to turn land over to the federal government: "I am sorry that such a story got out regarding the idea of establishing a National park and forest and game reserve in Missouri. The story as told in this clipping is so untrue that it won't do any good and may interfere with our operations in disposing of our lands, but I presume it will not receive very extensive circulation."[117] It is possible that the MLM could not ignore the potential for negative public reaction to mere rumors of federal land ownership in the Ozarks and reconsidered its strategies for disposing of cutover when confronted with adverse publicity.

White adhered to the Progressives' vision of conservation as wise use and promoted the efficient utilization of forests throughout the nation. According

---

[116] Grandin *Herald*, 10 May 1906.

[117] J. B. White to C. C. Sheppard, 14 February 1905, folder 11; and J. B. White to C. C. Sheppard, 27 February 1905, folder 12, both items in MLM Records. It is uncertain to which clipping White refers, because the Grandin *Herald* did not begin publication until 19 October 1905 and although the Van Buren *Current Local* was in circulation, it made no mention of the MLM donating or selling land to the federal government. Because White was writing from St. Louis, it is logical that a paper from that city produced the article, but I have been unable to locate the piece. Without this clipping in hand, it is difficult to make a strong conclusion on its significance.

to biographer John Galloway, White had begun to push for conservation by 1903. In 1905, President Roosevelt selected White to assess the status of the timberlands on Indian reservations in Minnesota. When White returned from this expedition, he recommended that the lands be carefully managed for the benefit of the resident Indians, rather than allowing private corporations to cut the timber. Although the industrialist operated his own mills strictly for profit, he continued to counsel the federal government on the importance of conservation. Missouri's Governor Hadley would also develop close ties with White in an effort to promote conservation in the state.[118]

As early as 1906, White began to plan for the MLM's future beyond Grandin. He shared his ideas for the company with some employees whom he regarded as friends and whom the company hoped to retain in its future ventures. White told his chief physician, Dr. Johnston,

> Regarding the future of Grandin, I think it is my duty to have a talk with you and Dr. Andrews when I come to Grandin, but I will say this now, that it will be safer to figure that there will be no town there in a few years. We have other plans which we hope to mature and I would not like to see my friends make any plans for the future of Grandin. I will ask you to keep this strictly confidential between yourself and Dr. Andrews, and I would like to have you tell Dr. Andrews not to mention it. We are not prepared to make public announcements of the plans of our company.[119]

The MLM viewed Grandin as a temporary home and felt no obligation to the region or its residents. By this time, White had expanded his interests in other Missouri counties and in Louisiana and had inspected forests in the Pacific Northwest for possible purchase.

In 1909, after years of declining profits, the MLM re-evaluated the costs and benefits of milling in Grandin. Once the company determined that the cost of transporting logs and ties to the community had reached a level where

[118] Galloway, "John Barber White," 164–89.
[119] J. B. White to Alexander Johnston, 17 March 1906, folder 133, MLM Records.

Figure 16: "At the end of the trail, 1909." This is the only titled photograph from the collection utilized in this study; WHMC assigned labels to the others for archival purposes (folder 1, p. 37, MLM Company Photographs, 1906–1916, WHMC–Columbia).

it would be advantageous to move the mill, it stopped new shipments of timber, drained the mill pond, and sawed all of the remaining logs on hand (see fig. 16). By October of 1909, the MLM had left Grandin for West Eminence in Shannon County.[120] As when the company had moved from White's Mill to Grandin in 1887, this was a short move to improve the company's access to timber and markets. However, the new mill would never match the production achieved at Grandin, and it would close after only a few years.

When the forests of Missouri no longer had enough timber to fuel the MLM's mills, the company picked up and moved to the less-exploited forests of the South. White carefully plotted the future of the MLM, even as he planned to transfer operations to other states. In 1909, Sheppard wrote White to request advice on how to handle the labor situation as the MLM

---

[120] J. B. White to C. C. Sheppard, 3 May 1909, folder 723; C. C. Sheppard to J. B. White, 9 August 1909, folder 733; and C. C. Sheppard to J. B. White, 22 September 1909, folder 737, all letters in MLM Records.

closed operations in Grandin. White responded, "You can explain to Mr. Willis and others that we don't need their services. But we may be able to give them work in the South later. But in the meantime they will not draw pay, we must stop Expense."[121] White worked to balance the company's needs for timber, transportation, and labor to generate the greatest possible profits. When these factors added up to insufficient gains, he made the decision to leave the Ozarks.

Almost a decade later, White was still struggling to divest himself of the remainder of his Ozark holdings. No longer desiring to control or maintain the company town of Grandin, he attempted to donate the entire community, including the company orchard in nearby Hunter, Missouri, to the educational board of the Congregational Churches of Missouri in 1918. The one stipulation proved too steep. White demanded that the churches create a "great industrial school in the town" named after himself. As with many of the company's efforts to permanently ensconce the world of industry in the region, this one failed due to a lack of local support.[122]

The rise and fall of the timber industry in the Missouri Ozarks brought many changes to the state. The manner in which the MLM and other companies utilized the region's forests was only one element of the transition for Ozarkers. The industry brought jobs, new communities, telephones, railroads, and a new vision of morality, and changed the economic and environmental bases of locals' culture. Although residents of the Courtois Hills made many efforts to maintain aspects of their pre-industrial lives, society had changed beyond their control. The MLM undoubtedly drew workers who were attracted by the increasing amenities of modern life in Grandin, but many of the common laborers hailed from the surrounding hillsides.

Even if no other changes occurred, Ozarkers' practices of subsistence agriculture, open-range grazing, woods-burning, and local use of timber would have had a much more significant impact on the forests with the increased population density by the beginning of the twentieth century. After the harvest of much of the region's woodlands, locals could no longer provide for themselves on plots of land with drastically diminished forest resources. The

---

[121] J. B. White to C. C. Sheppard, 13 August 1909, folder 733, MLM Records.

[122] Kansas City *Post*, 6 June 1918.

combination of increasing population and a booming timber industry led to a significant reduction in the quality and quantity of timber in the Ozark forests and left traditional Ozarkers with few economic options after the demise of the industry.

Chapter 3

The Means of Control
and Resistance

The first decade of the twentieth century witnessed great social conflict between large timber companies and many of their employees as each struggled to control the diminishing resources of the Courtois Hills. Those local residents, and their sympathizers, who desired to remain connected to their traditional lives were disenchanted with the social and environmental changes the timber industry brought to the region. At the same time, the timber companies were trying to make the greatest profit from the remaining resources. During that decade, Ozarkers and the MLM alike each intensified their efforts to achieve the society they desired.

These Ozarkers and industrialists clashed over their conceptions of how society should develop based on contrasting ideas of how to use resources.[1] One question that arises from this conflict is how these Ozarkers attempted to maintain elements of their pre-industrial lifestyles and relationships with the land and woods. Outsiders had several advantages in their attempts to gain control of the region, particularly money and legal authority. Residents of the Courtois Hills, however, used their possession and knowledge of the land, as well as their position as laborers, to shape the emergent industrial economy and society to meet their desires.

---

[1] This difference in attitudes towards resource use resembles situations described in Hahn, "Roots of Southern Populism"; and McMath, "Sandy Land and Hogs in the Timber."

Before the timber industry arrived in Carter County and the surrounding area, local residents held to a way of life rooted in generations of independence. The earliest white Ozarkers who settled in the more rugged areas chose small tracts of land along river valleys where they raised garden crops and relied on the surrounding woods for additional food and materials to build and heat their homes.[2] These Ozarkers inherited their cultural, social, and political affiliations from their ancestors, mostly Scottish and Irish immigrants who came to the area via the upland South, particularly the backcountry of Tennessee, Kentucky, and the Carolinas, as well as the frontier regions of western Pennsylvania. According to Donald Stevens, "Three-fourths of the adult settlers migrating to the southern Courtois Hills during the 1840s were born in the states of Kentucky, Tennessee, Virginia, and North Carolina. Only the Tennessee and Kentucky migrants, comprising about two-thirds of the 1850 population, traveled predominantly from their home state."[3] The first white settlers in the Ozarks were moving beyond the pale of Euro-American civilization; those who chose to settle in the most rugged regions developed a necessary independence and learned to flourish in isolation.[4] This situation prompted Ozarkers in the most isolated areas to develop trade and social relationships with a relatively small number of people in nearby areas.[5] The lumber companies sought to develop trade relationships with the outside world and to bring in new goods and ideas; many residents of the Courtois Hills whose independence was challenged by the timber companies' actions struggled to adapt to their new situation.

Pre-industrial life in the Ozarks rested on people's close relationships with their neighbors and with the land. Ozarkers' relationship with the Courtois Hills was one of non-intensive exploitation. Low population density allowed locals to utilize the woods without substantially degrading the hill country's ability to support future generations. The main way these Ozarkers altered their surroundings was through fire and open-range

---

[2] Gibson, "Living by the Land," 25–29.

[3] Stevens, *A Homeland and A Hinterland*, 24.

[4] Gerlach, *Settlement Patterns in Missouri*.

[5] For a selection of opinions on the Ozark culture of independence and isolation, see Randolph, *Ozark Mountain Folks*; Rayburn, *Ozark Country*; Gilmore, *Ozark Baptizings, Hangings, and Other Diversions*; Thelen, *Paths of Resistance*; and Blevins, *Hill Folks*.

grazing of their ever-present livestock, with woods-burning as a key element in the forest-subsistence economy of the Ozarks. Residents of the region established communities based on relationships with nearby friends and family and availability of natural resources most suitable to their needs, rather than on participation in markets for the sale of goods to outside markets. Although there were few economic connections beyond the Courtois Hills, the residents in the region freely participated in local exchange networks.

The Issue of Control

Once it established the company town of Grandin, the MLM earnestly began trying to direct people's lives and set the tone for changes in the region. Yet in spite of the company's efforts, residents of the town and the nearby hills forced the MLM to accept a series of compromises by creating an environment of interdependence between themselves and the company. These interactions suggest a complex relationship between local residents and the timber industry, whereby employees sought to maintain control of their society and the woods while timber companies sought to gain control of the workers and the forests.

The issue of control is a window through which one can view the actions of key individuals and groups in the conflicts associated with the Courtois Hills during the timber boom. Indeed, the idea of control, whether of hunting, land, or patterns of labor, has run through a number of influential studies of the South and of rural America. In the area of hunting, for example, conflicts over access to game in public lands between elite whites, who hunted for sport, and lower-class whites, who hunted for food, often left blacks, who were also in the lowest economic class, without access to the game animals they needed to feed their families.[6] Groups also clashed over control of the use of rangeland, with advocates of social and economic advancement fighting to enclose rangeland for private use and others fighting to maintain common grazing rights vital to small-scale or subsistence agriculture.[7] Control over labor emerged as a major source of conflict when industrialists attempted to bring pre-industrial people into a world based on productivity, punctuality, and efficiency.[8] All of these

[6] See Marks, *Southern Hunting in Black and White.*
[7] See, for example, Hahn, "Common Right and Commonwealth."
[8] See Gutman, *Work, Culture, and Society in Industrializing America.*

issues played out in the conflicts between Ozarkers and the MLM over who would determine the future of society and the woods in the region.

As the creator of Grandin and the employer of its residents, the MLM sought to transform society to meet its ideals. Company president White expressed his understanding of the town in a letter to William Warner, the Republican from Kansas City whom Missourians sent to the U.S. Senate in 1904: "Grandin is, as you are aware, a sawmill town. Our company, of which I am president, owns every house in it. It was started twenty-five years ago with a few houses and a sawmill, but to keep out whiskey and bad people we decided to build houses and not sell any land until we were all through with our manufacturing."[9] The MLM displayed a sense of righteousness as it tried to establish its idea of a perfect community in Grandin, despite any and all objections.

Control of Property and Related Economic Activities

Hunting presented many Ozarkers with an important social opportunity that crossed between economic strategy, traditional pastime, and leisure activity. Men who relied on the timber industry for their economic well-being often sought additional sources of sustenance for their families. Michael Kimmel argues that men who went from being self-sufficient as artisans or farmworkers to dependent wage laborers as industrial workers could no longer identify themselves as men based on their ability to determine their own schedules and to independently supply all of their families' needs. These men responded in part by creating their masculine identity through distinctive patterns of leisure.[10] Hunting offered men both a traditionally masculine leisure activity and an additional means of feeding their families. The combination of a diminished woodlands and new game laws, which were enacted by the first decade of the twentieth century, led many residents of the Courtois Hills to resort to trespass and poaching to feed their families.

By taking game, the MLM's employees regained some of their ability to ignore the company's attempts to control their economic position. The Grandin *Herald* regularly denounced those who violated game laws. In 1906, the paper condemned a man for fish bombing and a group of hunters for

[9] J. B. White to Wm. Warner, 29 January 1906, folder 80, MLM Records.
[10] Kimmel, *Manhood in America*.

violating the state's game laws while in Carter County. As a voice of reform, the newspaper called for convictions of those who refused to accept the middle- and upper-class notion of hunting as a sport rather than as a source of food.[11] During the late nineteenth and early twentieth century, reformers transformed hunting into a sport regulated by state agencies,[12] and the MLM undoubtedly held to this new idea of hunting. By 1893, the Carter County Fishing and Shooting Club, certainly not an association in favor of pothunting, began to show up as a regular entry in the company's account books.[13] Hungry residents of the hills, however, continued to see game animals as a much-needed source of food for their families.

Landholding Ozarkers could resist the MLM's control of the region by refusing to provide the company with the timber and land it depended on. By 1903, more than 213,000 acres of forest had fallen to the saws and axes of the MLM—approximately seventy acres per day when the mills worked at maximum capacity[14]—and the company was always searching for land with valuable timber and access to rail or river transportation. By 1906, the MLM was having difficulty obtaining land from individuals fully conscious of the company's needs. In regard to a particularly stubborn group of landowners, sales agent Charles C. Sheppard explained to White, "Mr. Webb [who served several terms as sheriff in Carter County] and Mr. Day spent a couple days along that line between Winona and Eminence and had a good effect. The farmers on Delaware Creek displayed considerable anxiety and some of them came to Mr. McGhee and asked him to close the matter up. Some of them reduced their prices by as much as $100.00."[15] There was no mention of Webb and Day's methods.

Once the company found valuable land, it had to find ways to bring the forests under its ownership. Landholders possessed a degree of agency not available to many of their neighbors. The players in this drama reveal much

[11] Grandin *Herald,* 20 September 1906, 22 November 1906. The conflict between the paper and poachers is similar to situations discussed in Warren, *Hunter's Game,* and Marks, *Southern Hunting in Black and White,* both of which deal with the social distance between elite and common hunters.

[12] Warren, *Hunter's Game*; and Marks, *Southern Hunting in Black and White.*

[13] Missouri Lumber and Mining Company account book, 1892–1893, vol. 85, p. 94, MLM Records.

[14] Galloway, "John Barber White," 163.

[15] C. C. Sheppard to J. B. White, 27 January 1906, folder 78, MLM Records.

about the interaction in the hills. Charles C. Sheppard was born in Missouri of two Virginia-born parents. Robert A. Webb's mother was from either Alabama or Tennessee, but both her husband and son were born in Missouri. William Day was most likely born in Kentucky to parents of the same state. James M. McGhee, a real estate agent in Grandin, was born in Georgia, as were both of his parents. The incident demonstrates that hill folk claimed extraction from across the upland South and chose their alliances with or resistance to the MLM as they saw fit, often with little connection to the length of time they had resided in the area.

The MLM also faced resistance to its efforts to control the economic resources of this corner of the Ozarks when locals chose to work under contract rather than through direct employment. When unable to meet its needs with its own loggers, the MLM arranged for farmers to supply Grandin with ties and timber.[16] In 1901 the MLM found it necessary to send "notices out among the farmers, offering an increased price for ties."[17] The company made the price hike temporary in an attempt to fill an immediate need for ties. Initially the increase was set for about one month, but after two weeks it was extended for another month to meet the company's needs.[18] Those area residents who had access to lands from which they could cut ties had a great deal of agency during the company's time of need.

Because many of the people with the skills and resources to hack ties preferred to remain relatively independent rather than work directly for the company, the MLM was often forced to purchase ties from local farmers even when it had timber on its own lands. This situation allowed residents of the Courtois Hills to extract higher prices for their ties. At one point Sheppard explained to White, "For the last four months we have been making all the red oak ties we could get made along our Shannon County tram. We have not succeeded in getting many red oak ties up to this date. Most of them have been made by farmers from their own timber, and have cost us 18 [cents] per tie."[19] White replied that "it may pay us to put in our portable

---

[16] According to Lon Horgan, a resident of the region born in 1883, a man could hack ten to twelve ties per day on average. He noted twenty ties in a day as a personal maximum. See Horgan, interview.

[17] J. B. White to C. E. Slagle, 10 June 1901, vol. 9, p. 118, MLM Records.

[18] J. B. White to Missouri Lumber & Mining Co., 13 June 1901, vol. 9, p. 145, MLM Records.

[19] C. C. Sheppard to J. B. White, 30 August 1906, folder 222, MLM Records.

mill somewhere in Shannon County, and we will consider it as soon as the road is finished."[20] This was probably not the only time local residents seized an element of control over their own lives and the MLM chose this method of dealing with the resulting problems.[21]

During its tenure in Grandin, the MLM worked to maintain a strong hold over dissenting voices. When Daniel Huett, an attorney born of Missourian parents, assisted several Ozarkers who objected to the MLM's suits to force rights-of-way across their land, the MLM took immediate action. White explained his response to a friend: "We thought it cheaper to get rid of his opposition by retaining him for the year."[22] The MLM had the means to solve their problems by simply buying their opponents' attorneys away from them.

With its economic resources, the company had a distinct advantage over most Ozarkers in the legal arena. One of the MLM's consistent expenses was a local attorney, Mr. Livingston, whom it kept on retainer. In 1906, White had Sheppard send Livingston a check and explained, "Say nothing about this to anyone, because neither Mr. Livingston nor myself want it known that he is in our employ. He will do us more good in discouraging litigation by not having it known that he is employed by us."[23] That the MLM felt the need to keep this arrangement secret suggests a great deal about the social environment of the region. Company employees and residents of the surrounding area did not trust the MLM and would not accept the opinions of an attorney in its employ. The company also felt no compunctions over the use of deceit in manipulating its workforce.

The Contest for Social Control

By courting risk through economic wagers and rejecting company restrictions, employees expressed their independence in their leisure time through gambling. Locals engaged in the activity as much more than an opportunity to dispose of free time; it allowed men to sit in the company of others and communally reject unwanted social boundaries. The MLM responded by diligently working to rid

[20] J. B. White to C. C. Sheppard, 8 October 1906, folder 245, MLM Records.

[21] Hall, *Like a Family*, 33, 39–40, 147, discusses a similar situation in the company towns of the cotton industry.

[22] J. B. White to Hon. Louis F. Dinning, 3 January 1900, vol. 3, p. 383, MLM Records.

[23] J. B. White to C. C. Sheppard, 22 September 1906, folder 232, MLM Records.

its communities of gambling. One clear authority the company exerted in its battle against gambling was the control of space. Chief cashier Fred W. Wright suggested to J. B. White, "I believe it would be advisable to have the Spread Eagle house near the Y— torn down, as it has lately been made a rendezvous by gamblers etc."[24] Wright proved a loyal functionary for the company, possibly due to his own and his wife's migration to the community from the MLM's home state of Pennsylvania.

A week after receiving Wright's missive, White wrote to Howard Davis, a mill foreman in Grandin, "I understand the prosecuting attorney has made some arrests for gambling. This will be a good thing if they can break it up. It may throw you out of the use [of] a few men in the start but it will save you trouble in the future."[25] Davis, who refused to divulge his or his parents' birthplace to the census taker, seemingly complied. White hoped—in vain—that a few arrests would scare his employees off from what he considered a vile pursuit. Risking hard-earned money on mere card games and other such entertainments demonstrated ideals that differed from those of the MLM. Many locals did not define their activities by the overriding drive to accumulate wealth through gainful labor; rather they freely risked money for entertainment.

The circuit court records for Carter County provide another glimpse into gambling in the Ozarks. Between 1890 and 1920, the circuit court heard only four cases for gambling (none from the 1904 incident), even though the MLM and reformers considered it one of the most pressing social problems the Grandin area faced. This difference suggests the inability, or unwillingness, of county officials to indict or convict locals for gambling.[26] There were many, however, who enjoyed the inherent camaraderie and risk involved and refused to give it up, or to report or convict their fellow gamblers.

The MLM was not unique in its attempts to wipe out gambling among its workers. In the fast-growing commercial center of Rochester, New York, local

---

[24] F. W. Wright to J. B. White, 15 February 1904, folder 2, MLM Records. Wright, his wife, and their parents were all born in Pennsylvania. It is unclear whether the Wrights had known the company's founders in Pennsylvania.

[25] J. B. White to Howard Davis, 22 February 1904, folder 2184, MLM Records.

[26] Circuit court records for Carter County, 1871–1934. These records are most accessible in the county history files of the Missouri State Archives in Jefferson City.

leaders criminalized gambling in the 1820s, but found they could not enforce the legislation, so they decided to compromise by taxing gambling instead.[27] According to Gunther Peck, gambling had an important role among miners in the late nineteenth-century boomtown of Virginia City: "Prize fights and gambling contests nonetheless formed important elements of an alternative working-class culture in Virginia City, one that venerated chance and limited economic gain rather than rational capital accumulation."[28] Throughout the nation, gambling was often at the intersection of subsistence or pre-industrial and profit-driven cultures.[29] Reformers attempted, almost always to little or no effect, to control vices through whatever means were at their disposal.

The administration of the various churches in Grandin demonstrates the difficulties the MLM faced in its efforts at social control. In 1907, White wrote to E. B. Grandin, "The Congregational Church [the religious institution patronized by company leaders] has been doing, and is doing the best work in Grandin. The Methodist Church has not got over half the membership of the Congregational Church, and while the Baptists take the lead in numbers, yet their progress has been stimulated by the Congregationalist Church in Grandin." White then painted a picture of the emergence of middle-class propriety in the Baptist Church: "Their bare walls and tobacco stained floors and walls, oftentimes with sawdust on the floor for the benefit of tobacco chewers—have been given up because of the example set by the Congregational Church in putting in nice pews and in carpeting and papering their church."[30] Despite the Baptist Church's move towards the image of "civilization" that White desired, the company continued to favor the Congregational Church. The Baptists accepted some changes in their favored religious institution, but continued to stay away from the sanitized righteousness of the Congregational Church.

---

[27] Johnson, *Shopkeeper's Millennium*, 71–72. For another discussion of the importance of gambling as a leisure activity for working-class males, see Rosenzweig, *Eight Hours for What We Will*, 55.

[28] Peck, "Manly Gambles," 79.

[29] Many studies demonstrate the centrality of gambling in the social unrest that accompanied the arrival of industry. For two examples of failed attempts at eliminating games of chance, see Murphy, *Mining Cultures*, 119–20; and Johnson, *Roaring Camp*, 279, 284–85.

[30] J. B. White to E. B. Grandin, 6 September 1907, folder 584, MLM Records.

Education was another arena of conflict between the MLM and many area residents. It is uncertain what percentage of local children attended the Grandin public school or from how wide an area these students came, partially because of the state's lax compulsory education laws. The few graduating classes of Grandin's high school mentioned in the records during the MLM's tenure in the community consist of approximately four students per class. There is evidence that locals did not meekly concede control over education in the region to the MLM. The fate of the school building, which burned to the ground at least twice, in November 1905 and January 1909, hints at the unrest caused by company control of education. On both occasions, the newspaper suspected arson, conjecturing in 1905 that "the fire is supposed to have been of incendiary origin."[31] These incidents suggest a level of tension between divergent views of the role of education. As the MLM attempted to instill the values of industrial America into the minds of the community's youth, parents may have felt a growing cultural distance from their children. Carter County had an illiteracy rate of roughly 30 percent immediately before the arrival of the MLM, and while there was undoubtedly a sizable portion of the population that agreed on the importance of education, many in the vicinity obviously did not consider compulsory education necessary.[32]

Tension between those in favor of and those opposed to reform in the Courtois Hills also appeared in the different ways these groups viewed the consumption of alcohol. The company's approach to alcohol use among its workers reflected its patriarchal practices. Though whiskey flowed when White entertained guests in Grandin or at "the clubhouse" on the Current River, the MLM felt it had the knowledge and right to determine proper behavior for its employees and therefore banned alcohol and anything else that interfered with an individual's ability to work.[33] Grandin was not unique in its conflict over alcohol. In his study of southern manhood, Ted Ownby noted, "Despite the popularity of swearing, shooting, and animal fighting, it is clear that drinking and drunkenness were the most popular recreations in southern towns. Men drank while enjoying other recreations, or drank as

[31] "School House Burned," Grandin *Herald*, 9 November 1905; and "Recommendation of Board of Trustees of Library Assn.," no date, folder 6913, MLM Records.

[32] See the 1880 U.S. Census for Carter County.

[33] For one example, J. B. White to Wm. Sander, 31 November 1907, folder 639, MLM Records.

their sole recreation, drank at large gatherings, or in small groups."[34] The issue of alcohol use pervaded the conflicts in Grandin between industrial-minded reformers and those hill folk and others who chose recreation over labor.

The case of Dr. C. Rhea provides one of the best illustrations of the MLM's attitude towards alcohol use among its employees. Although the company held doctors in high regard, not even they were immune to the MLM's efforts to rid the town of what it considered an efficiency-destroying evil. In 1906 the MLM hired Dr. Rhea, a resident of Oregon County, to fill in for its physicians who were on vacation. Shortly after the hiring, Sheppard was forced to inform White that the new doctor "returned from his trip among the loggers over near Ellington in an intoxicated condition." This simple imbibing with the loggers set in motion a series of actions, as Sheppard explained: "We were immediately notified of the fact and Dr. Roth was sent from Store #8 to Store #9 camp that night. Dr. Blount was sent from here to Store #9 camp Sunday afternoon via Van Buren, to relieve Dr. Rhea and he came in to Grandin yesterday." Sheppard immediately fired Rhea and promptly sent him "home on today's train."[35] Away from the oversight of the company, Rhea had decided to enjoy the camaraderie and whiskey of some of the MLM's loggers. When he came out of the woods and into the realm of the company's cultural influences, however, he was reminded that the MLM had no tolerance for any of its employees wasting time inebriated.

Although such heavy-handed control did not go unchallenged, the MLM continued to attempt to control its employees' use of alcohol. When Sheppard discovered a source of whiskey that was being bootlegged into a company logging camp, he wrote to White to propose bringing in federal marshals to stop the flow.[36] White replied, "Let Sheets or Clark [minor company officials] write U.S. Marshall. You don't want to figure in it personally."[37] White realized that if the employees considered Sheppard responsible for bringing federal marshals to the camp to prosecute local bootleggers, the manager would lose what support he enjoyed. Despite its efforts, the company could not

[34] Ownby, *Subduing Satan*, 50.
[35] C. C. Sheppard to J. B. White, 16 June 1906, folder 189, MLM Records.
[36] C. C. Sheppard to J. B. White, 9 December 1905, folder 46, MLM Records.
[37] J. B. White to C. C. Sheppard, 14 December 1905, folder 46, MLM Records.

completely end its employees' alcohol use, but it did combat conspicuous use. The MLM refused to hire individuals with a history of drunkenness and fired anyone caught bootlegging or intoxicated, even when employees engaged in these activities while away from the job. The company also encouraged churches to promote sobriety and sponsored social associations with temperance tendencies.[38] The company's frequent disciplinary actions for the use of alcohol indicate a continuing desire by residents of the region to reject the company's vision of society as devoted to sober and efficient production.

Local residents often sought to supply themselves and their friends with bootlegged alcohol despite the MLM's strenuous objections. In Van Buren, the county seat of Carter County, local officials arrested Bill Parker on charges of being a public nuisance. The details of the case reveal that the court suspected Parker of "harboring a blind tiger." The term "blind tiger" was used in the early twentieth century for an illegal drinking establishment because owners of illicit saloons often placed stuffed tigers with glass eyes in their legitimate businesses as an invitation to potential patrons. Local officials had grown to accept Parker's poolroom (his legitimate business), but could not condone a known source of liquor in their community.[39]

The MLM's employees in the Courtois Hills consumed alcohol, primarily whiskey, regardless of the consequences. At one point Sheppard informed White, "I have learned today that our Planing Mill Foreman, Chas. Pennington, who is a brother of the Foreman of the Planing Mill at Clarks [LA], has been drinking considerable whiskey, and I discovered that he had taken whiskey to the Planing Mill on one or two occasions and had hidden his bottle away in the Patterns Room upstairs." Sheppard also noted that the man's work "has not been altogether satisfactory."[40] Although Pennington held a position of responsibility for the MLM and undoubtedly understood the consequences of his actions, he drank on the job until the company caught and fired him. Without overstating this instance, it does represent yet another

---

[38] C. C. Sheppard to J. B. White, 9 December 1905, folder 46; J. B. White to C. C. Sheppard, 29 January 1906, folder 80; C. C. Sheppard to J. B. White, 19 June 1906, folder 189; C. C. Sheppard to J.B. White, 15 December 1909, folder 743; and Bylaws of the Grandin Athletic and Band Association, Gymnasium, no date, folder 6909, all items in MLM Records.

[39] Grandin *Herald*, 12 July 1906.

[40] C. C. Sheppard to J. B. White, 15 December 1909, folder 743, MLM Records.

occasion on which the MLM and one of its employees in the Courtois Hills clashed over the appropriate use of alcohol.

Other than violence, bootlegging was probably the most persistent problem the company faced. Many in the Courtois Hills readily made alcohol available to their neighbors and escaped into the woods when the company attempted to force them to stop. In June 1908, the *Herald* noted, "Sheriff Gunn, Constable Hiltibidle, T. M. Lawhorn, and W. C. Gunn made a raid on some Bootleggers who were operating on Current River. They captured the men and seized about two gallons of whiskey."[41] Even though bootleggers were fined, they continued to distribute their product; circuit court records for Carter County demonstrate a regular stream of bootlegging and offenses related to drinking. Making and consuming whiskey offered those who opposed the company an opportunity to declare their independence from the vision of society the MLM promoted.

The meaning and perception of violence was another area affected by changing ideas of society and gender. Reformers in Grandin recognized that violence often occurred as a demonstration of masculinity. The Grandin *Herald* stated:

> There is a certain class of people who think it a proper thing to carry a gun. In their minds they would not be men if they did not have a gun or some other weapon on their person with which to settle any dispute that might come up or some grudge that might exist. In our opinion such creatures are cowards, low down, dirty contemptible cowards, who haven't the least spark of manhood in their make-up.[42]

Violence often sprung up as a crucial point in the differing ideas of manhood in the area. Employees and residents of the surrounding hills refused to give

---

[41] Grandin *Herald*, 11 June 1908. Unfortunately it is difficult to conclusively identify these men other than the constable. Robert S. Hiltibidle was born in Illinois and lived in Carter County from at least 1900 to 1910. An examination of U.S. Census records demonstrates that Gunn was a common name among farmers and day laborers in Carter County. Lawhorn was less common, though a number of families in the Courtois Hills shared the name.

[42] Grandin *Herald*, 31 May 1906.

up their freedom to own, carry, brandish, and fire weapons. This uniquely masculine entertainment offered an obvious method of establishing manliness and independence.

Much of the nightly gunfire in Grandin and the surrounding area led to no serious injury and was a prime outlet for the tensions of men who engaged in a physically difficult and dangerous occupation. In June 1906, the *Herald* noted, "We understand that a bunch of warrants have been turned over to the constable for the arrest of the pistol toters who persist in shooting up the town at all hours of the night."[43] Although warrants were issued, there is no indication that any arrests were made. This suggests either the unwillingness or the inability of the constable to carry out his duties. Because the constable maintained a close relationship with the MLM, it is unlikely that he did not intend to assist the company in its efforts to bring peace and productivity to Grandin. It is more likely that he found it difficult to arrest individuals who partook in what locals considered acceptable behavior. Communities throughout the nation that were on the cusp of the industrial system often became fertile grounds for violence.[44]

These pistol toters refused to let the issuance of warrants ruin their fun. In 1907 the *Herald* opined, "The fellows who shot off their revolvers a few nights ago immediately after some young ladies had passed them on the main sidewalk, deserve both a fine and imprisonment for carrying concealed weapons."[45] This episode suggests a great deal about Grandin. The location, on the main sidewalk, is important. If young men could stand in the middle of town and fire off revolvers without being prosecuted, a large segment of the population must have been indifferent to, or cowed by, the behavior. Although the intentions of the fellows in question were never stated, two main possibilities exist. It is possible that the men merely sought the young ladies' attention and this was their version of a catcall. Just as likely, however, is the possibility that the men were exerting their control over a public space—the main street—at night, by declaring themselves dangerous men who should be feared.

[43] Grandin *Herald*, 28 June 1906.

[44] See, for example, Johnson, "Bulls, Bears, and Dancing Boys," 63–64; Murphy, *Mining Cultures*, 48–49; and Hyde, *Pistols and Politics*.

[45] Grandin *Herald*, 14 March 1907.

The *Herald* made opposition to the carrying of weapons one of its main causes. A March 1907 issue editorialized, "If the sheriff wants to make some fees or wants to make a record for himself as an officer, we suggest he start right here in Grandin and make a crusade against the fellows who are never known to be without a gun or a dangerous knife upon their person." The same article continued, "We will venture the assertion that if he would search every fellow whom he sees upon the streets after eight o'clock at night, that he would find either a gun or a dangerous knife upon at least three out of five."[46] Because a significant element of the community refused to change their lives to fit reformers' visions of modernity, nightly gunfire remained a common part of life in Grandin. By carrying and firing guns, residents of the community forcefully rejected the social agenda of reformers.

Much of the gunplay in the area occurred with little personal injury, but armed confrontations were not unknown. The records seem to demonstrate frequent instances when the relatively small number of women in the timber towns were caught in the crossfire between the communities' lonely men. In 1906, both William Eastham and Charles Stacy sought the affection of Rose Ezell. Eastham and Stacy each became enraged when Ezell told them, individually, of rumors she had heard that disparaged their reputations. In response, William and his two brothers, George and Willis Eastham, confronted Stacy outside a local church. Both sides were armed and took umbrage at what they believed the other had said. In the ensuing gunfight, Stacy killed Willis Eastham and injured George Eastham before he himself was mortally wounded. William Eastham was the only man to escape unharmed. George Eastham was arrested and faced murder charges, but almost escaped when someone smuggled a saw into the prison, which he used to cut through the bars of his cell.[47] This case was dramatic and public enough to warrant legal action, which left a valuable trail of records. The willingness of Charles Stacy and Willis Eastham to settle their dispute with firearms suggests a preexisting level of unrest in the region. It is likely that the men placed their efforts at conflict resolution in a context that was accepted, though not by the MLM, to at least some degree in the region.

[46] Grandin *Herald*, 14 March 1907.

[47] Grandin *Herald*, 31 May 1906, 2 August 1906, and 29 November 1906. It was not uncommon to find women at the center of violent conflicts in resource-dependent communities that were new to industrialization. For an example, see Murphy, *Mining Cultures*, 87.

There were several other cases of murder or attempted murder in the region with a diverse range of circumstances. Harry Numbers shot and wounded Cora McGriff, the half-sister of his dead wife, in what Numbers and McGriff called a case of jealousy. When Numbers went before the judge for the incident, the Grandin *Herald* noted, "The woman in the case, who was shot and was the chief prosecuting witness, has married the defendant and refused to testify and the case was dismissed."[48] It seems as though the couple subsequently found the Courtois Hills an unwelcoming place, as the 1910 census places them in Numbers' home state of Illinois. The case could illustrate the casual occasion of violence or the oppression of a woman by a violent and unstable man. In either instance, the case points to the unsettled nature of society in Grandin as violent individuals clashed with reforming elements.

Other cases emphasize how random the consequences could be when violence was so common. On one occasion, a local farmer, J. L. Abrams, was in the town of Winona on business when he was shot and killed accidentally by a randomly fired bullet. At the turn of the century, the Courtois Hills was a region undergoing a great deal of strife connected to its transition to an industrial economy and company-dominated society. Even residents of the hill country who tried to remain independent of the timber companies had to do business in towns where violence often reigned.[49]

Violence occurred at all levels of society in Carter County. The most dramatic and public cases found their way into local newspapers where editors denounced the perpetrators. The circuit court records for Carter County present another picture. Between 1880 and 1920, the court heard at least 120 different cases stemming from episodes of violence. This category includes murder, rape, assault, carrying a concealed weapon, and a host of other crimes. Men were the perpetrators of every one of these violent crimes.[50] The frequency of violence and the fact that it remained the sphere of men provides insight into the region. A visible portion of the male population rejected the dictates of reformers and timber companies, claiming power through the use of firearms and by forcibly imposing its will on its neighbors.

[48] Grandin *Herald*, 26 July 1906, and 27 September 1906.
[49] Grandin *Herald*, 18 October 1906.
[50] Circuit court records for Carter County, Missouri State Archives, Jefferson City.

Conflict in the Workplace and the Realm of Productivity

Employees unhappy with the role of the company extended their acceptance of violence as a means of dispute resolution into their conflicts with the MLM. Frequently stymied in their attempts to achieve a sense of economic and social independence through peaceful means, employees took their frustrations out on the symbolic institutions of the company. In addition to the two episodes of burning down the schoolhouse, locals vandalized railroads and the company store. As connections to modernity and the industrial world, these institutions symbolized the changes the company had brought to the Courtois Hills.

The MLM's railroad, its lifeline to the outside world, stood out as a visible symbol of its reach throughout the region. Occasionally vandals attacked the railroad by placing obstructions on the tracks, such as in 1905 when an engine derailed after running over a chain (fig. 17). As in most cases, the perpetrator was never found.[51] Generally, however, railroad crews noticed and removed obstructions before accidents occurred. In 1907, Sheppard described to White a series of acts of vandalism:

> During the week of December 4th we had some trouble on our Shannon County tram near our Store #9 camp in Horse Hollow on account of some obstructions being placed on our track. Our steel gang was gping [*sic*] out on the North Main line when they went to work and the engineer noticed a log lying in the middle of the track and saw it in time to stop the train and remove it. They went up to their work and later in the afternoon had to return to the camp for some water and on their return trip found some angle bars laid on the rail. They discovered this in time to stop and remove them in time not to derail the train. Proceeding a little further they found a spike driven between the joints of the rail and discovered this in time to remove it without accident. The next day one of the men

---

[51] C. C. Sheppard to J. B. White, 8 September 1905, folder 138, MLM Records.

Figure 17: "Train Wreck Near Grandin, 1907" (folder 2, p. b, MLM Company Photographs, 1906–1916, WHMC–Columbia).

in our section crew found a short piece of steel rail laid on the track but he removed it before the train passed that way.[52]

These actions posed a serious problem for the company in terms of productivity and safety. Individuals who targeted the railroad extended the cultural acceptance of violence in their society to their protests against the changes the company brought to their lives and woods.

Sheppard felt obligated to make a strong reply to the challenge. He informed White, "I sent Mr. Hiltibidle up there and after spending two or three days on it he found that two young men had done this work." Sheppard continued, "After Sim [Hiltibidle] gathered sufficient evidence he arrested these two young fellows and they admitted to him in the presence of witnesses that they put the obstructions on the track." The primary responsibility resided with a twenty-year-old named Conway. In identifying Conway, Sheppard stated, "He worked for some time driving a team but his work was not satisfactory, and as Hanson [his supervisor] could not get him to

[52] C. C. Sheppard to J. B. White, 19 December 1907, folder 693, MLM Records.

do a good days [*sic*] work he discharged him and he has not worked in any other departments since that time. We understand that he was pretty angry because he had been discharged." Sheppard then told White, "We thought best to make an example of these young fellows and Hiltibidle filed information against them at Eminence, and they have been arrested and put in jail there."[53] The MLM undoubtedly saw this as a serious challenge to their authority in the region and worked to ensure that it would not happen again.

Unfortunately, we do not have Conway's side of the story. All that we can say is that the Conway in question was probably C. H. Conway, born in Missouri in 1882, who appears in the 1920 census for Carter County as a teamster hauling wood. The events point to another case of divergence between the MLM and its employees as to what constituted a sufficient work ethic. As a teamster, Conway performed the difficult and dangerous job of handling horses and mules in the rugged Ozark terrain. The MLM relied on railroads to get logs to the mills and lumber to the market, but animal power was needed to get logs to the rails and onto the cars. The company's combination of traditional and modern power sources included at least eleven mule teams and two teams of oxen (fig. 18).[54] When the company insisted that Conway increase his productivity beyond a pace he found appropriate, he refused and MLM responded by firing him.[55] If this is the same Conway who placed obstacles on the rail tracks, he serves as an example of actions a local worker might take in attempting to retain control of his own life by lashing out with any available opportunity when industrialism threatened his traditional lifeways.

The MLM's actions in dealing with accidents demonstrate its understanding of its workforce. The company provided relief to some injured workers, but only when they professed loyalty. Profits remained much more important than employees' safety in the eyes of the company. When a Mr. Snider complained about the safety of his job, White told Sheppard:

[53] C. C. Sheppard to J. B. White, 19 December 1907, folder 693, MLM Records.

[54] Missouri Lumber and Mining Company account book, 1881–1882, vol. 50, pp. 100–112, MLM Records.

[55] There is an extensive, though dated, literature on the difficulties people have faced when adapting to the rigors of industry. For a selection of examples, see Thelen, *Paths of Resistance*; Gutman, *Work, Culture, and Society in Industrializing America*; and Kulik, "Dams, Fish, and Farmers."

Figure 18: Mule getting off train car (folder 2, MLM Company Photographs, 1906–1916, WHMC–Columbia).

After such a complaint has been made by Mr. Snider I believe it is unsafe for us to have Mr. Snider work at that kind of work, and I wish you would have a talk with Mr. Snider and see if you cannot get him to take another job. I am afraid that there will be a serious accident and as Mr. Snider has called our attention to this, if there should be an accident it is going to be made expensive for us.[56]

It is unclear who Mr. Snider was, but there is a good chance he was from a long line of Ozarkers. With six Sniders listed as head of household in Carter

---

[56] J. B. White to C. C. Sheppard, 4 December 1905, folder 45, MLM Records.

County in the 1870 census, it was the most common surname in the county.[57] When employees tried to effect change within the company, the MLM made its priorities apparent—profits sat above all other concerns.

Two particular injury cases demonstrate another aspect of the relationship between the MLM and its employees. In 1889, Mike Carmody approached the main mill's large circular saw as it was slowly coming to a stop so he could sharpen the teeth. Through what appears to have been complete negligence, the sawyer moved the pin that controlled the log carriage's progress. Because of this action, the carriage began to creep toward Carmody and the saw. Another mill employee saw the impending danger and "hollered." Carmody heard the shout, saw the carriage, and jumped for safety. As he leaped, his foot struck the carriage, sending his knee into the saw blade. Carmody was immediately transported to the company hotel where a doctor amputated his leg, but despite medical attention, Carmody died shortly thereafter.[58]

The attitude of the MLM towards its employees and their response is evident in the injuries of Mike Carmody and James Parker. In one of the statements the MLM collected regarding Carmody's accident, a coworker stated, "Mr. Carmody was what is known as a 'rusher,' and was always anxious to make his work show up well."[59] James Parker worked for the MLM feeding wood into a lath mill until part of his hand was cut off as he tried to clear away some sawdust that was inhibiting the machine's performance. In his statement, Parker claimed "that the Lath Mill was out of repair; ... and that the Mill Foreman, Mr. A. R. Commins would not allow Jas. Parker to raise the tightner [sic] and stop the saw; and that A. R. Commins had given him a task of 16000 Lath per day; and if he stopped the Mill he could not have made the number of Lath, and would have lost his job."[60] Carmody climbed the carriage tracks and stood in front of a still-spinning saw in order to demonstrate his industriousness. Parker lost his fingers because he was forced to meet a quota

---

[57] U.S. Census Office, *1870 U.S. Census Population Schedules*.

[58] Statement of George Nanna, 11 November 1889, folder 6726; Statement of S. B. Leeper, 17 November 1889, folder 6727; and Statement of Sarah Carmody, 11 December 1889, folder 6726, all items in MLM Records.

[59] Statement of Frank Arnold, 14 November 1889, folder 6727, MLM Records.

[60] Statement of James Parker, presented by G. W. Akers, 6 October 1892, folder 6730, MLM Records. Parker dictated his statement concerning the loss of a portion of his hand to Akers, who recorded and presented the injured man's version of the events.

that prevented him from taking necessary precautions to clean his equipment. These two cases demonstrate the MLM's power over its workforce and its rejection of safety standards to protect its employees. The cases also show the tragic results that awaited many of the workers who succumbed to the MLM's demands rather than fight back or protest as Mr. Snider did.

As the owner of the company store and the landlord and employer of all residents in Grandin, the MLM set prices, rents, and pay rates to ensure profitability. The year 1907 is a good example of how the company dealt with economic problems, as it was a minor depression in the timber industry nationwide. The company store (fig. 19) gave the MLM the ability to artificially discount wages, as it did in 1907, when it paid workers in checks and planned to take care of the next payday with credit at the store.[61] Later in that year, Sheppard replied to White's proposal to set wages as low as possible: "If any of our men should leave us, in case you make this reduction in wages, we would have no trouble in getting others to take their places."[62] The MLM had the ability and the desire to manipulate the labor situation to meet its needs—a situation its employees seemed to recognize and resent.

Figure 19: "The Company Store" (folder 2, p. a, MLM Company Photographs, 1906–1916, WHCM–Columbia).

---

[61] J. B. White to W. W. Warren, 16 November 1907, folder 661, MLM Records.

[62] C. C. Sheppard to J. B. White, 19 December 1907, folder 667, MLM Records; and Grandin *Herald,* 9 January 1908.

One tool available to the company in its efforts to manipulate its labor force was the hospital association. Such an association may at first glance seem an unmitigated good, but not all Ozarkers agreed. When typhoid fever struck the town in 1906, a company employee, R. W. Cook, enlisted the services of a doctor from outside the community because he felt the company's physicians were not giving his stricken daughter the proper care. When Cook's daughter died despite the additional treatment, he asked the MLM for assistance with his doctor bills on the grounds that he had been paying into a fund for medical treatment. The MLM refused, claiming the hospital association, which was the recipient of his payments, was a completely independent institution, and that the company merely collected the payments for the association.[63] Despite this claim, it is clear that the MLM had established itself as the only source of treatment for injury and sickness, a situation that gave the company power over the workers and expanded the workers' dependency on the company. This case also demonstrates the MLM's lack of sympathy for individuals who turned to other sources for help.

One problem White noticed in Grandin was the frequency of sickness in the community. He lamented to Sheppard, "For some reason it takes more medical attention to look after our Grandin plant than it does in Louisiana." He determined that "at Grandin it would seem to indicate that the Missouri climate requires more physicians than does that of Louisiana."[64] On the same day, White observed to Johnston, "At our mills at Clarks, Fisher, and Victoria, La., we do not have nearly the amount of sickness that we have at Grandin." White then surmised, "I believe from observation at Grandin and from observation at the other mills that there is a much larger percentage of employees who go to the hospital for medical treatment at Grandin than our other mills. They have gotten into the habit."[65] There is a hint of resistance in the employees' readiness to declare a sick day rather than go to work. Perhaps White was subtly urging Johnston to be wary of workers' claims of illness.

The use of sickness to resist the modernization of society is a firmly documented tradition. Throughout the nation such social conflicts followed the

[63] C. C. Sheppard to R. W. Cook, 1 September 1906, folder 224, MLM Records.

[64] J. B. White to C. C. Sheppard, 30 January 1905, folder 8, MLM Records.

[65] J. B. White to Dr. Alexander Johnston, 30 January 1905, folder 8, MLM Records.

growth of industry. In his study of Rochester, Johnson found that laborers often "spent Sunday drunk and Mondays visiting their friends." Johnson demonstrates that individuals uncomfortable with factory labor often turned to the company of their friends and family instead of following the dictates of industrialists demanding production.[66] This tendency may explain the high rate of sickness White commented on in Grandin.

As part of its efforts to keep its employees working, the MLM prevented the formation of unions and suppressed any outward support for striking among its laborers. In 1906, several Southern timber companies formed the Southern Lumber Operators' Association to prevent and put down strikes. White wrote to W. W. Warren (the general manager of the affiliated Louisiana Long Leaf Lumber Company of Fisher, Louisiana) to inform him that the MLM would subscribe to the association: "Of course it should be jept [sic] quiet that we are taking any means to help our brother members in those strikes. We would not like it to appear there was a large fund being raised for this purpose."[67] The MLM never had to draw on the fund, but White was prepared for a strike, showing that despite the company's efforts, it never obtained complete control over its workforce. The MLM's numerous efforts to keep employees and locals cooperative suggests consistent resistance. The MLM would not have spent so much effort or income on maintaining its hold on labor if it did not feel it was necessary.

The pace of work and the occasion of holidays were frequent causes of labor unrest in Grandin.[68] After generations of operating within a subsistence and local exchange economy, locals were not prepared to make a rapid transition to the work of industrialized logging and milling, and resisted such annoyances as a workweek that included Sunday. Residents of the Courtois Hills also fought companies who tried to operate their mills on holidays such as Christmas Eve. The conflict over who controlled the pace and hours of work was a consistent thread throughout the history of the timber boom in the Missouri Ozarks.

Sunday labor proved to be a particularly difficult issue between the MLM's devotion to profits and many employees' pre-industrial traditions. Local

---

[66] Johnson, *Shopkeeper's Millennium*, quote at 42.

[67] J. B. White to W. W. Warren, 6 October 1906, folder 232, MLM Records.

[68] On the issue of holiday labor, see Rosenzweig, *Eight Hours for What We Will*, 65, 68–70.

residents considered Sunday a day of rest and refused to give up what they considered an important aspect of their lives. When the company expanded into Reynolds County, it included Sunday in the workweek, but Ozarkers objected to the loss of their day of leisure. When Sheppard informed White of the problem, the company's president responded, "If even the occasional running of a log train in Reynolds County is an offense to the citizens, explain the result to our men and we will stop it."[69] A few months later, in need of production, the MLM once again attempted to undertake Sunday work. White told Sheppard, "Replying to yours of Jan. 11th regarding working on Sunday in Reynolds County. I would suggest that it might be well for you to see Prosecuting Attorney Sloan and have a talk with him." White continued, "If you talk with Mr. Sloan you could tell whether you would want to recommend paying him $300.00 a year attorney fees. We would like the privilege of calling on him when we had anything to do, that is, providing when you see him you think he is of sufficient caliber to be influential enough with the people so that we would not be prosecuted for doing necessary work on Sunday."[70] There is no indication of whether the company made the offer or whether Sloan accepted the retainer. But despite the MLM's efforts, the company did not succeed in opening Reynolds County to Sunday work over locals' objections.

Shortly after expanding into Reynolds County, the MLM extended its tramlines in Shannon County and again ignored local tradition and the state law mandating a day of rest on Sunday. The prosecuting attorney for Shannon County responded, "I have been reliably informed that you are continuing to work on Sundays in the construction of your railroad and tram road in Shannon County. This being in violation of Section 2240 of the Revised Statutes of Missouri of 1899, you will therefore refrain from continuing such work on the Sabbath."[71] Sheppard relayed the charges to White and told him, "We suppose there is nothing we can do at present, except discontinue this work, but it will make it pretty hard for us to do at all times."[72] The issue of work-

[69] J. B. White to C. C. Sheppard, 17 July 1905, folder 32, MLM Records.

[70] J. B. White to C. C. Sheppard, 12 January 1906, folder 69, MLM Records.

[71] G. S. Sizemore to Missouri Lumber and Mining Company, 11 February 1907, folder 364, MLM Records.

[72] C. C. Sheppard to J. B. White, 11 February 1907, folder 364, MLM Records.

ing on Sundays was a significant point of conflict in the struggle over who would control the hours of work and leisure. Despite resistance, the MLM considered the extra workday important enough that they continued to doggedly pursue Sunday labor. This was one of the few conflicts where residents of the region were able to successfully appeal to county officials through the legal system. It is possible that these challenges succeeded because they were contested outside of Carter County. Shannon, Reynolds, and other neighboring counties hosted a strong timber industry, but escaped utter domination by corporations more successfully than Carter.

The End of Grandin's Heyday

As it planned to close its mill at Grandin due to the depleted forests, the MLM demonstrated the character of its relationship to the town and its workers. By 1907, the MLM decided to stop paying workers in cash and switched to company checks and credit, redeemable at the MLM's store. White noted that the company "posted notices that we can pay no currency, and that if our employees insist on waiting for cash for their services we shall shut our mills down."[73] A week after discussing the postings, White told W. W. Warren that the MLM "expects to have to pay them [the workers] their next pay day in orders on our grocery."[74] This coupon system left the employees in a difficult situation. During this episode, Sheppard noted that the MLM's locomotive machinist stated "he had some money on hand and some of the men were willing to discount checks to him if he would cash them." Sheppard continued, "The men would be very foolish to pay him anything to cash the checks for them but there are some who will do it, just as there are men who will draw our coupons and sell them at a discount of from ten to twenty percent."[75]

After years of trying to make ends meet on company wages, the MLM's employees had a new problem in the summer of 1909 when the company began to inform the workers that their services were no longer needed.[76] The Grandin mill closed in the fall of 1909 with no advance warning for the

---

[73] J. B. White to Miss May Wilson, 7 November 1907, folder 653, MLM Records.

[74] J. B. White to W. W. Warren, 16 November 1907, folder 661, MLM Records.

[75] C. C. Sheppard to J. B. White, 16 November 1907, folder 661, MLM Records.

[76] J. B. White to C. C. Sheppard, 13 August 1909, folder 733, MLM Records.

majority of the company's workers, who had no chance to plan alternative economic strategies.

Many former employees found themselves in desperate straits when the company left. As the MLM prepared to leave town, Dr. Johnston wrote to White expressing his concern for the people left behind. The record indicates that a group of residents appealed to Johnston for economic assistance as the MLM was leaving Carter County. White replied to Johnston regarding "the cases of suffering you mentioned":

> When we move away from Grandin we will, of course, not move these people. I note this class of people drift in from the surrounding country where there are public works, and they are doubtless encouraged to come by others who sympathize with them. … It is singular that we have so many of these cases at Grandin, and I hear of none at any of our other mills in Louisiana. I think that there is less poverty and less suffering among the white people of Louisiana than there is in southeast Missouri; doubtless there is a good reason for it.[77]

White expressed his philosophy clearly. He felt that any economic problems in the region were solely the fault of people who chose to settle there. He encouraged his friend to accept this social Darwinism and allow these impoverished folks to fend for themselves.

Once the MLM made public its plans to leave Grandin, locals were concerned about how they would adjust to life without the timber industry. In a letter to Dr. Johnston, White wrote an impromptu monologue he claimed to have delivered when some employees confronted him at the company store. White wrote that he told the crowd that he

> considered it much better for them to have a small farm and a garden even if they lived in small log houses and raised their living and have their hogs fattening on the mast, that they would be better off than working around a sawmill and paying rent,

[77] J. B. White to Alex Johnston, 18 January 1910, folder 753, MLM Records.

that only those account of some fixed expense that is going on
all the while whether they work or not, while if they have a small
garden or a small farm they have something growing and are
paying no rent.[78]

This statement departed from the company's earlier depiction of Grandin
as an idyllic community with all of the amenities of modern life. When the
company needed workers, it enticed them with promises of more modern
living. When it pulled up stakes, White assured Ozarkers a subsistence-level
agrarian lifestyle would be more fulfilling.

The efforts of the MLM to establish a modern city in the most rugged
portion of the Missouri Ozarks brought it into direct conflict with residents
of the region and employees who accepted paychecks, but chose not to blindly
follow company perceptions of thrift, hard work, and social responsibility.
Outwardly, the MLM maintained control of resources, politics, religion, education, and the economy. Employees, however, refused to give up their own
lives. Workers never went on strike, but they did force the MLM to alter its
attempts to institute industrialism in the area. When the company called
for Sunday work, people throughout the area turned to their elected county
officials to protect their interests. When the company refused to pay workers in cash, employees found an entrepreneur willing to cash their company
checks. Hill folk, whether employees or not, rebelled openly when they perceived railroads or schools as challenges to their visions of society. As control
of society oscillated between employees and reformers, those caught in the
middle frequently turned to violence to settle disputes. The MLM's efforts to
shut off alcohol use produced a pervasive and persistent trade that remained
beyond its control. As the company attempted to shape society to reflect its
values of propriety and productivity, it found the limit of its powers when it
ran up against the desires of regular workers and contract employees who had
different conceptions of the area's proper social and economic development.

---

[78] J. B. White to Alexander Johnston, 5 February 1910, folder 755, MLM Records.

Chapter 4

Resistance to Governmental Involvement in the Ozarks, 1905 to 1931

During the first three decades of the twentieth century, the Ozarks continued to witness major social and environmental changes. As the timber boom ended, the Courtois Hills fell into economic depression and the state and federal governments failed to overcome resistance to their proposed conservation policies. Governmental visions of forest policy remained beholden to industrial benefactors. Missouri, however, made its initial steps towards establishing a resource policy for fish, game, and parks during those decades.

At the national level, conservation had become a major topic of discussion shortly after the Civil War, and new conservation policies produced some significant results. The federal government responded to fears of resource depletion by changing its land policy in an attempt to sustain future stores of natural productivity. By the late 1870s, the federal government began to seek ways to limit the rampant abuse of public domain lands nationwide. In 1876, Franklin B. Hough became the first man hired by the federal government to investigate the nation's forests and determine potential courses of action. The German-born forester Bernard Fernow then took over for Hough in 1886 and rapidly increased the scientific underpinning of the study of the nation's forests. Fernow successfully ensconced forestry as a division within the U.S. Department of

Agriculture shortly after his appointment.[1] Forestry continued to evolve within the federal government and by the beginning of the twentieth century became a concern of widely recognized importance. Wildlife conservation also emerged at the federal level during the late nineteenth century with the creation of the U.S. Biological Survey and passage of the Lacey Act of 1900, which prohibited the interstate transfer of illegally taken game.

Another important factor in national conservation at the turn of the century was the emergence of progressivism. The Progressives fought to bring efficiency and rational management to natural resources and social programs. One of the key Progressives in the field of conservation was Gifford Pinchot. In 1898, he began to serve as head of the federal division of forestry, the agency that would become the U.S. Forest Service and gain control of the nation's forest reserves in 1905. Along with the growing influence of Pinchot, Theodore Roosevelt's rise to the presidency marked the arrival of progressivism as the driving philosophy behind national resource policy. At the turn of the century, natural resource policy, including forestry, was directed by a desire to conserve resources through management to enable present and future generations to extract the greatest possible sustained yields.[2]

Missourians' acceptance of effective conservation policies generally lagged behind the creation of national policies. Because of the efforts of the state's sportsmen, Missouri was able to begin enacting legislation to support wildlife conservation in the first decade of the twentieth century, though it would be decades before the state would devote significant resources to the cause. In terms of effective forest conservation, however, Missouri was about three decades behind the federal government and at least as tardy in comparison to most other major timber-producing states. Missouri's slower pace resulted in part from resistance by some residents in portions of the Ozarks, such as the Courtois Hills, to governmental influence.

Governor Folk and Early Forest Conservation Efforts

One key to the successes for early conservationists in Missouri was the rise of Joseph W. Folk to the governor's seat in 1905, where he served a single four-

[1] Williams, *Americans and Their Forests*, 394–401.
[2] Hays, *Conservation and the Gospel of Efficiency*, 121–25.

year term. Folk infused the state's government with the reformist spirit he had demonstrated as prosecuting attorney in St. Louis, where he was fearless in defending consumers by prosecuting corruption. Folk and his successor, Herbert Hadley, brought their own versions of national progressivism to the state's government. While governor, Folk worked with industrial leaders and sportsmen to promote conservation and to make resources available to the greatest number of Missourians. He emerged as the pioneering force behind the state's attempts to undertake conservation.

As early as 1905, the state legislature began to express interest in gaining control of Missouri's natural resources for the public good. In that year, the General Assembly approved a bill proposed by Harry R. Walmsley, a representative from Kansas City, to protect the state's game animals. One of the more controversial measures in the Walmsley Game and Fish Law was its ban on the sale of game meat. It also established a system of game wardens in the state's employ, began the sale of licenses for hunting and fishing, regulated seasons for hunting game animals, and protected nongame species in the state. Missourians were temporarily open to government regulation in 1905 as they recognized that their game animals were disappearing, and they placed much of the blame on market hunters who supplied meat to visitors to the 1904 World's Fair in St. Louis.[3] This law gave Missouri a foothold in the control of its natural resources.

Whether Missouri's early attempt at regulating the state's game was successful or not, it did establish a philosophical base for later efforts. In his first annual report (1905) to Governor Folk, the state's new game warden, J. H. Rodes, expressed another key element of the Walmsley Law: "Under the new game law ownership of the birds, fish and game in Missouri is declared to be in the State and is held for the benefit of the people in common."[4] Rodes epitomized the conservationist ethic of the Progressive era. The office of the state game warden, created by the Walmsley Law, operated under the assumption that enlightened individuals could determine how to use resources to provide the greatest good for the greatest number of people. Implicit in this

[3] Callison, *Man and Wildlife*, 7–8.

[4] Rodes, *Annual Report of the State Game and Fish Warden… 1905*, 30. The annual reports of the state game and fish commission are held in the Missouri State Archives in Jefferson City.

philosophy is the understanding that some individuals would disagree and that the state would possess the power to punish lawbreakers.

The sale of hunting licenses is one example of how the state attempted to control people's relationships with nature. In his 1907 report to Governor Folk, Rodes introduced an accounting of the sales of hunting licenses, a standard feature of subsequent reports. He noted that in 1906, Carter, Reynolds, and Shannon Counties (all in the Courtois Hills) each accounted for fewer than twenty licenses. The proportion of the population holding licenses in these counties was also quite small. Based on the 1900 population count, one in about three hundred Carter County residents had a license. The smallest ratio of licenses to population was in Shannon County, based on the 1910 census, when one in about 1,500 Shannon County residents held a license. In the majority of other counties throughout the state, residents purchased at least one hundred licenses, with the residents of some counties applying for over one thousand.[5] Subsequent annual reports continued to demonstrate this trend. The Courtois Hills remained well behind most of the rest of the state in the purchase of game and fish licenses during the first decades of the twentieth century. The failure of the residents of these counties to purchase licenses suggests they may have recognized the system as an attempt by the government to increase its control in the region and thereby reduce free access to the bounty of the woods. It is also possible that many simply refused to acknowledge the expansion of state power into this area of their lives.

The reluctance of the residents of the Courtois Hills to purchase hunting licenses was not unknown to state officials. As reported by the Missouri Game and Fish Department, in 1909, "[Jacob] May [of St. Louis] was the first man to buy a hunting license in Shannon County." This action so surprised the local sheriff that he told May, "If you go out hunting with that thing I'll have to arrest you."[6] The story may be apocryphal, but it speaks to the attitudes of many of those who chose to make the rugged hill country their home.

The state's efforts to gain control of its game populations and, by logical extension, to reduce the opportunities to hunt enjoyed by many hill folk,

[5] Rodes, *Annual Report of the State Game and Fish Warden… 1907*, 6–8; U.S. Bureau of the Census, *Twelfth Census*; and U.S. Bureau of the Census, *Thirteenth Census*.

[6] *Missouri Game and Fish News* 4, no. 1 (January 1928): 14.

proved to be a major source of conflict. Hunting was a long-standing tradition that many Ozarkers had carried with them through the middle Atlantic states and upland South from their ancestral lands in the British Isles. Marks points out that hunting held a place of great cultural importance for Scots-Irish immigrants to the Carolinas in the early and mid-eighteenth century.[7] Because many residents of the Courtois Hills came from this stock of people, it is important to recognize that the state government was attempting to regulate an activity that, for many, was imbued with close to two hundred years of cultural significance.

The state government was aware of the resistance it faced in the area. In 1907, Rodes reported to Governor Folk, "Unquestionably the greatest hostility to the present game law eminated [*sic*] from the south and southeastern part of the State."[8] Rodes worked against an entrenched system that favored Missouri's rural citizens and market hunters. Much of the success in fighting game laws emerged because of the way Missouri selected its state legislators. Each of Missouri's 114 counties was guaranteed at least one representative, with the remainder of the House of Representatives' 142 members divided between the state's major metropolitan areas. This system awarded rural voters a disproportionate amount of power in comparison to voters in urban areas, a situation that continued to become more severe as Missouri's rural population declined and its urban population increased. As an example, in 1900, six representatives spoke for the over 575,000 people in the city of St. Louis, or one representative per approximately 95,833 people. The 6,700 residents of Carter County in 1900, on the other hand, had the sole claim on the attentions of their representative, George T. Lee.[9] Missouri's legislators listened to their constituents and replaced the Walmsley Law with a dramatically weaker piece of legislation in 1907.

The key year for conservation during the Folk administration was 1908, during which the first assessment of the state's timberlands was published and Folk committed Missouri to conservation on a national stage. Samuel J. Record, who would become forest supervisor for the Ozark National Forest

---

[7] Marks, *Southern Hunting in Black and White*, 34–35.

[8] Rodes, *Annual Report of the State Game and Fish Warden… 1907*, 45.

[9] List of members of the Missouri House of Representatives in the section identifying the members of the Fortieth General Assembly, in *Official Manual of the State of Missouri… 1899–1900*, 170–71.

in Arkansas when it was established on 6 March 1908, assessed Missouri's timberlands in 1906 and published his report in 1908. Although the ultimate motivation for the project is unclear, the College of Agriculture at the University of Missouri claimed credit as the initial driving force for an early survey by Record.[10] It is possible the university was interested in promoting a national forest that would include land in both the Missouri and the Arkansas Ozarks. It is also likely, however, that the U.S. Forest Service initiated the study. In his report, Record demonstrated a deep concern for the future of Missouri's forests. He determined that 60 percent of the state had been forested at the time of the first European settlement. He estimated that due to destructive timber harvest and woodland fires, however, only 35 percent of Missouri was forested as of his 1906 survey. Worried about the future of the Ozark forests, he warned Missourians that, at their current pace, they would strip their state of its pine forests by 1913 and of all marketable timber by 1918.[11]

Many forestry officials of the early twentieth century, such as Record, turned to similar and often-unsubstantiated rhetoric of an impending timber famine. Record made his claims for the dire future of Missouri's forests despite his admission that "it is to be regretted that there are no reliable estimates as to the total present stand of merchantable timber [in Missouri]."[12] Record's recommendation that Missourians work with the U.S. Forest Service to establish national forests in the state went unheeded for almost thirty years. His report, however, coincided with the first stirrings of sentiment in favor of forest conservation in Missouri.

The 1908 Conference of Governors in Washington, DC, proved to be a seminal event for forest and waterway conservation throughout the nation. According to the organizers of the conference, President Theodore Roosevelt had first floated the idea of the meeting in a 1903 speech to the Society of American Foresters. He argued, "The relation between forests and the whole mineral industry is an extremely intimate one. The very existence of lumbering depends upon the success of our work as a Nation in putting practical forestry

---

[10] Westveld, *History of Forestry*, 4.
[11] Record, "Missouri's Opportunities in Forestry," 2, 7.
[12] Ibid., 1–5.

into effective operation."[13] By 1907, Roosevelt had become convinced that "the conservation of our natural resources and their proper use constitute the fundamental problem which underlies almost every other problem of our National life."[14] This conference was the first instance when the president assembled all of the governors to address a single issue of national concern. It also solidly placed conservation in the political realm. Roosevelt urged each governor to recognize that it was no longer sufficient to let scientists, professionals, and sportsmen bear the responsibility for maintaining resources for future generations. The politicians acknowledged their responsibility and the meeting was a rousing success.

President Roosevelt invited each governor to bring up to three advisors. Governor Folk selected John A. Ockerson, William H. Black, and N. W. McLeod to join him.[15] Ockerson, a St. Louisan, was a well-known civil engineer by the time of the conference. During the 1890s, he had served as the senior engineer for the Mississippi River Commission; in 1904 he was the chief of liberal arts exhibits at the World's Fair in St. Louis; and in 1912 he would be elected by his peers as president of the American Society of Civil Engineers. Ockerson certainly brought a wealth of experience and concern with waterways to the delegation. Black seems a less obvious choice in that he was president of Missouri Valley College in Marshall, a Presbyterian minister, and a professor of psychology and ethics. Although Black had no overt connections to conservation, he would remain a key figure in Missouri's efforts to establish forest policies in the state during the first two decades of the twentieth century. The third advisor, N. W. McLeod, is more of a mystery, though he was a lumberman from St. Louis who had already, by 1898, "been friends for a great many years" with J. B. White.[16]

Missouri's representatives played a significant role in the meeting. On the afternoon of 14 May, during the fourth session of the conference, Governor

---

[13] Theodore Roosevelt, address to the Society of American Foresters, 26 March 1903, quoted in "Origin and Plan of the Conference," in Blanchard et al., *Proceedings of a Conference of Governors, 1908*, v.

[14] Theodore Roosevelt, address to the National Editorial Association, 10 June 1907, paraphrased in "Origin and Plan of the Conference" in Blanchard et al., *Proceeding of a Conference of Governors, 1908*, vi.

[15] "Roster," in Blanchard et al., *Proceedings of a Conference of Governors, 1908*, xxii.

[16] J. B. White to N. W. McLeod, 7 November 1898, vol. 1, p. 328, MLM Records. The best genealogical match for McLeod is a banker named Nelson McLeod with parents from Scotland and Maine.

Folk had the opportunity to address the assembly. In a short speech that was interrupted by applause and shouts of support at least fifteen times, Folk identified his positions on the issues of forest and waterway conservation. He even chose to wander into some controversial territory: "I have been wondering why, if it be so necessary to preserve our forests, it would not be a good idea to put lumber on the free list—make lumber free [from tariffs]. I hope that it is not heresy. It seems to me that for every foot of lumber brought here from another country we preserve a foot of lumber in our own forests." Opposition to this point was offered, but quickly squelched in favor of maintaining the conference's strict schedule. In addition to calling for national action, Folk vowed, "As soon as I go back [to Missouri] I am going to appoint a State Forestry Commission."[17] The governor carried through with his intentions and on 1 December 1908, he created the Missouri Forestry Commission.[18] Folk's participation in the conference was his first significant move in his efforts to bring conservation to Missouri.

William H. Black, whom Folk would appoint to the Missouri Forestry Commission, also addressed the conference, albeit from a different view. He spoke from the perspective of recreation rather than game management: "It is highly important … that watersheds and shore lines be reforested in the interests of game and fish supplies." This is significant because the dominant strategy of managing game populations at the beginning of the twentieth century was to eliminate undesirable species while stocking the preferred game species. The idea of managing game populations through habitat protection would not become widespread until several decades later. It is misleading, however, to attribute to Black the status of environmental prophet. Black considered himself a proponent of nature for its aesthetic and restorative powers: "Hunting and fishing are our finest forms of recreation, and thousands of lives are bettered by the open air, the change of scene, the mental excitement, and the good fellowship of hunting and fishing."[19] His commitment to the importance of forests and streams as resources for urban sportsmen would become

[17] Folk, "Address by Joseph W. Folk, Governor of Missouri," in Blanchard et al., *Proceedings of a Conference of Governors, 1908*, 159.

[18] Von Schrenk, "Report of the Missouri Forestry Commission," sect. 48, p. 3.

[19] Black, "Conservation From the View-Point of Recreation," in Blanchard et al., *Proceedings of a Conference of Governors, 1908*, 371–72.

a significant issue of contention when he served on the forestry commission with individuals devoted to maintaining forests as storehouses of timber.

The Missouri Forestry Commission began amid an impressive state and national commitment to conservation, yet it fell short of establishing state forestry in Missouri. The original members—Dr. William H. Black; Dr. Hermann von Schrenk, a forestry expert; David A. Latchaw, a Kansas City newspaper editor; and W. E. Barns, a St. Louis newspaper editor and timber industry spokesman—served *pro bono*, hoping to make a difference rather than a paycheck.[20] Folk pushed for forest conservation throughout his time as governor, but he never gained the popular support necessary to implement his programs. The forestry commission, however, did follow Folk's lead and attempted to move the state towards the creation of a sustainable forest policy.

Deforestation coupled with fire prompted Folk to push for effective forest conservation. He discussed the consequences a sick timber industry could have on the general welfare of the state in his valedictory biennial message in 1909, stating: "The destruction of our forests by waste and fire should alarm all thinking citizens." Folk's fear was that the misuse of the state's forests would leave Missouri without "a foot of lumber left" within twenty-five years. Although he did not absolve timbermen of responsibility, he argued, "The greatest enemy of the forest is not the axe, but fire."[21] The governor, like Record, employed the rhetoric of timber famine to gain public and industrial support for his programs. By placing fire above harvest as the main problem Missouri's forests faced, it seems that Folk recognized the power of industrialists and urban sportsmen. This suggests that Folk saw residents of the rugged portions of the Ozarks who burned their forests as being more destructive than timber corporations that recklessly high-graded the state's woodlands.

Despite growing concern over the health of the state's forests, efforts to protect Missouri's game and fish still dominated governmental conservation. As the state attempted to increase its control of its resources it had to expand its "protection" staff. In 1909, the Missouri Game and Fish Commission

---

[20] For more extensive biographical information on Black, see Woodruff, "William H. Black"; for Barns, see Marquis, *Book of St. Louisans*, 39; and for Latchaw, see *Who's Who in Kansas City, 1930*, 113.

[21] Folk, "Message," 16–17.

employed twenty-one "regular deputy game and fish commissioners," stationed mostly in Missouri's cities, as well as fifteen "extra deputy game and fish commissioners," whom it placed where help was needed, in the smaller Ozark communities of Poplar Bluff, Salem, Doniphan, Ellington, Van Buren, and Rolla. The commission also deemed it necessary to employ two individuals to detect "fish dynamiters" in Poplar Bluff and Doniphan.[22] The ability to take game in Missouri's forests was an early issue dividing government and many who chose to live in the Ozarks.

Many families who made their homes in the more rugged areas of the Ozarks depended on game animals for subsistence. The memories of two residents from the banks of the Big Piney River reflect the local importance of gathering game from the land. Corky Hargis, born in the Ozarks in 1928, stated that without rabbits, squirrels, and fish, her family would not have been able to make ends meet in the 1930s and 1940s. Ferrel Dablemont, born in the Ozarks in 1927, tells a similar story. He remembers trapping and fishing as the means of survival during the 1930s and 1940s.[23] Those who depended on free access to animal resources for subsistence were in direct conflict with the state government, which sought to protect natural resources for the good of the whole public.

Governor Hadley's Conservation Efforts

Missouri's initial commitment to its forest resources, in contrast to its fish and game populations, was short-lived. In 1909, the National Conservation Commission convened in Washington, DC, and Missouri's forestry commission printed its report. Both of these events would demonstrate that Missouri had begun to lose interest in forest conservation.

The meeting of the National Conservation Commission in Washington, DC, illustrated some of the problems forestry's supporters faced in Missouri. Governor Herbert Hadley, Folk's successor, reappointed the state forestry commission but was stymied in his efforts to promote forest management in Missouri. John A. Ockerson, Dr. Hermann von Schrenck of the state forestry commission, and three members of Missouri's waterways commission,

---

[22] Tolerton, *First Annual Report*, 3–4.

[23] Robert Hargis and Corky Hargis, interview; and Ferrel Dablemont, interview.

including William H. Black, attended the National Conservation Commission as delegates from Missouri. Champ Clark, a powerful veteran member of the U.S. House of Representatives, and J. B. White served as official members of the national commission's forestry board. In this second national meeting on the subject of conservation, no Missourians made speeches or took part in any vigorous debates on record. Missouri had seemingly lost its desire to stand in the front rank of the nation's conservationists.[24]

This meeting is one of the early occasions where White's name appears in connection with Hadley's and with conservation. White and Hadley were two of Kansas City's most prominent citizens and each voted the Republican ticket. This may have been enough to bring the men into the same social circles, but their commitment to conservation certainly brought them together. Although he continued to exploit the forests of the Missouri Ozarks with wanton disregard, White had established a notable record as an advocate of conservation from the position of progressivism by 1909. In the following years, he would continue to advise the federal government on conservation and push for more efficient use of the nation's forests.[25]

After spending its first year (1908/09) studying forests throughout the state, the Missouri Forestry Commission produced a series of recommendations in late 1909:

1. a permanent forestry commission
2. a complete survey of the state for quantity and quality of timber
3. a program of public education in support of forestry
4. changes to the current tax laws
5. a firefighting and prevention program
6. a state-sponsored nursery
7. the ability to accept and manage lands for forestry
8. a source of permanent and substantial funding

These recommendations mirrored the requests Folk had made two years earlier. The Missouri Forestry Commission placed itself squarely in the midst of progressivism with a series of proposals calling for the efficient management

---

[24] Frederick Dunlap to Dean Mumford, 15 December 1913, folder 366, Dunlap Papers. And see Gannett, *Report of the National Conservation Commission, February 1909*, 28, 30, 116. For biographical information on Clark, see "Champ Clark," unprocessed clippings file at SHS Ref. Libr.

[25] Galloway, "John Barber White," 163–89.

of resources to benefit the public. At the heart of these recommendations and the progressive ideology of conservation was a call for the support of the development of scientific forestry.

Despite the commission's best efforts, its recommendations failed to resolve some critical issues, such as the purpose of forestry in Missouri. Latchaw attempted to include the management of city and town parks under the aegis of the commission's proposed Division of Forestry. Barns and von Schrenk worked against Latchaw's efforts, proclaiming that such a measure "does not directly pertain to a bill intended to promote forestry, a matter entirely distinct from parks."[26] The issue may seem minor, but its implications were momentous. A forestry program synonymous with park management would invariably emphasize recreational and aesthetic values. If the state devoted its proposed forestry agency to the economic values of woodlands, however, it would more likely develop as a supply agency for timbermen. The commission's inability to solve this issue left Missouri without direction in its efforts to create a unified forestry policy.

The commission also failed to reach a conclusion on the crucial issue of forestland taxation: "We [the commission] wish to call further attention to the fact that we have dealt but briefly with what we consider the most important phase of the entire question, viz., the problem of taxation. We did this because we felt that this also is a debatable point." The commissioners argued that although a remedy for inequitable taxation was necessary, they did not have enough information to make a recommendation. The issue of forestland taxation appeared throughout the nation as each state addressed the concerns of forest conservation. Traditional property taxes are inequitable when applied to forestland because a forest taxed every year only rewards its owner with a harvestable crop about once in a generation, even when managed well. In contrast, an agricultural field, under expected conditions, produces an annual crop to at least reduce the tax burden. Ordinary real estate taxes give an incentive to landowners who clear-cut their woodland and let the land revert to the state or county for back taxes rather than pay annual fees.

The inability of the commission to reach a decision on the benefits of legislative restrictions on timber cutting also reflected the philosophical divisions

[26] Von Schrenk, "Report of the Missouri Forestry Commission," sect. 48, p. 4.

within the board. Black argued for well-defined measures to protect forests, while Barns and von Schrenk opposed restrictions as they again represented the interests of timbermen. The latter two men argued, "We are endeavoring to create a sentiment for conservation in the State of Missouri, and in order to do this, it seems wise to advocate only such policies as are clearly practicable ones, and furthermore, only such policies as are unquestionable."[27] The conflict within the commission revealed the problems inherent in establishing a forest policy for Missouri. The commission was unable to determine whether Missouri's forests would be devoted to supplying the needs of industrialists or to the aesthetic demands of the state's growing urban population. The governor's handpicked committee recognized the need for action, but was unwilling to brave controversy in a state still resistant to the expansion of governmental power.

In the early years of the movement to conserve forests, the state gained many opportunities from the owners of large cutover parcels who sought tax relief. In 1909, Governor Hadley appealed to the legislature to support the commission's recommendation for a bill to authorize the state to obtain land for conservation. Hadley explained, "I am advised that the owners of large tracts of land in the southern half of this state from which the timber has been cut would be glad to deed the same to the State for such purposes [reforestation to check erosion]."[28] Although Hadley left the landowners unnamed, it is undoubtedly more than a coincidence that 1909 was the same year in which Hadley's associate White was moving the MLM out of Grandin. C. C. Sheppard informed White on 22 September 1909, "We will finish taking out all of the logs that it will be profitable for us to take out by next Monday or Tuesday at the latest, and can finish sawing them and be ready to commence taking down the mill by the first day of October."[29]

The efforts to secure favorable policy for the conservation of Missouri's forests forced key leaders such as Hadley to choose where they would invest their time. In August 1909, Hadley declined, though with regret, an invitation to a national meeting of conservation commissions in Seattle. He

[27] Von Schrenk, "Report of the Missouri Forestry Commission," sect. 48, p. 12.

[28] Hadley, "Waterways and Forestry Commission," 6–7.

[29] C. C. Sheppard to J. B. White, 22 September 1909, folder 737, MLM Records.

stated, "I doubt very much if I will be able to attend at that time [August 1909]; however, I should be very glad indeed to have the members of the Waterways Commission and also the members of the Forestry Commission attend."[30] Most notable among those who attended the meeting was J. B. White, whom Hadley personally selected.[31] About a year later, Hadley again had to choose between two important activities. When W. E. Barns requested Hadley's presence at a Missouri Forestry Commission meeting to be held in St. Louis on 30 October, the governor responded, "I regret very much indeed that on account of the fact that I expect to leave St. Louis on October 25th for a trip down the river with President Taft, it will not be possible for me to attend this meeting."[32] The governor often found himself sending his regrets to conservationists because of demands on his time.

Despite the challenges he faced, Hadley continued to assist Missouri's conservationists in their efforts to protect the state's forests. He took the initiative to set up a tour of the Ozarks with Gifford Pinchot and the Missouri Forestry Commission for 1910, but had to withdraw in the early stages of the planning. At the time, Pinchot was the acknowledged leader of forest conservation in the United States. In addition to serving as the first chief of the U.S. Forest Service, he had helped found the Yale Forestry School, which sent some of its students to Grandin to gain practical experience with the Missouri Lumber and Mining Company in 1906. After Hadley withdrew from the excursion with Pinchot, the governor turned responsibility for the trip over to J. B. White, who had a standing relationship with Pinchot.[33] Both were nationally known conservationists, had served together at the National Conservation Commission, and had a record of personal correspondence.

The proposed Ozark tour apparently never happened. Many possible explanations exist but the occurrence of the Ballinger-Pinchot controversy is one of the most intriguing. When President Taft appointed Richard A. Ballinger as

---

[30] Herbert Hadley to W. W. Kavanaugh, 30 June 1909, vol. 10, p. 373 (roll 5), Hadley Papers.

[31] Galloway, "John Barber White," 165–67.

[32] Herbert Hadley to W. E. Barns, Secretary of the Missouri Forestry Commission, 9 October 1909, vol. 17 (roll 10), Hadley Papers. It is unclear whether President Taft made the trip.

[33] Herbert Hadley to Capt. James B. White, 2 February 1910, vol. 13, p. 207 (roll 7); Herbert Hadley to Gifford Pinchot, 12 March 1910, vol. 13, p. 543 (roll 7); and Herbert Hadley to James B. White, 14 February 1910, vol. 13, p. 308 (roll 7), all in Hadley Papers.

secretary of the interior, the new cabinet member and Pinchot clashed almost immediately. In 1909, Ballinger supported the transfer of coal-rich lands in Alaska to private corporations. When the incident came to Pinchot's attention, the forester objected to what he judged to be an underhanded maneuver that would deprive the larger public of the benefits of the lands. The ensuing confrontation resulted in Pinchot's dismissal in January 1910 on charges of insubordination. The charges emerged from Pinchot's attacks on Ballinger's character in the press and on the floor of Congress.[34] Pinchot's loss of political position during the planning stages for the Ozark tour posed a potential problem. The former chief forester suddenly found himself thrust into a nationwide debate and a political maelstrom. Pinchot's political volatility may explain Hadley's decision to withdraw from the excursion and place responsibility in White's hands. The new challenges and demands may also have left Pinchot unable to meet his commitment in Missouri.

Although Hadley attempted to advance conservation in Missouri, he was unable to make significant progress. There is no definitive single explanation, but two possibilities seem likely. One possibility is suggested by the important role of White and other industrialists in activities such as the conservation commission and the proposed float trip with Pinchot. Hadley may have relied on industrialists for support and been unable to establish policies counter to their needs. Timbermen who remained in Missouri after the boom attempted to determine the direction of forest conservation in order to maintain profits. One result was the disinclination of Hadley and other conservationists in the first two decades of the twentieth century to consider the needs and desires of those who lived in the wooded, and formerly wooded, Ozarks. This is the second likely reason Hadley failed to succeed in launching conservation programs. Because Ozarkers generally only achieved recognition in early conservation discussions in the negative context of woods-burning, they had little reason to support the efforts of a government that did not seem to have their interests at heart.

From the printing of the Forestry Commission's first report in 1909 to the founding of the Missouri Forestry Association in 1921, there were no fewer than ten different forestry bills introduced into the General Assembly,

[34] Hays, *Conservation and the Gospel of Efficiency*, 166–70.

with none obtaining the support of both the legislature and the governor. Professors at the University of Missouri, industrial leaders, members of the forestry commission, Missouri sportsmen, and the governor all participated in sending forestry bills to the state's legislators.[35] The legislature and the governor each backed forestry measures, but not the same ones. Because they disagreed with one another and lacked the support of the public, Missouri's conservation leaders were unable to bring pressure to bear on the state government and bridge the legislative gap.

Woods-Burning and the Open Range in the Cutover

A small group of influential individuals sought policies for the conservation of Missouri's forests in the first three decades of the twentieth century, but the creation of a governmental presence in the Ozark woods faced stiff resistance by residents of the lands in question. Even optimistic boosters of state forestry, such as Samuel Record, recognized the difficulties forest managers had to contend with in the Ozarks.

> My advice to the people of Missouri, on the forestry question, is to begin at once, but proceed slowly. The methods of a century cannot be revolutionized in a day, and it cannot be expected that a people, who for years have been busy destroying the forests, should suddenly concern themselves with forest protection and tree planting. This change must come about gradually, but because of the slowness of the movement, there is all the greater reason for immediate action.

Record acknowledged the damage the timber industry had wrought on the Ozark forests, but farmers who remained in the region and regularly burned the woods bore the brunt of the blame in his assessment.[36] Despite the reform efforts of several individuals, including some Ozarkers, rural Missourians refused to give up their generations-old dependence on the woods. They and

---

[35] For examples of bills introduced into the General Assembly, see f. 195, Dunlap Papers; von Schrenk, "Report of the Missouri Forestry Commission," sect. 48, p. 13; "An Act Creating a Forestry Board," sect. 48, p. 15; and Herbert Hadley to W. E. Barns, 14 January 1911, vol. 17, p. 289 (roll 10), Hadley Papers.

[36] Record, "Missouri's Opportunities in Forestry," 4–6.

the politicians who supported their interests may have feared that forestry legis-lation would lead to further interference with their traditions of woods-burning and open-range grazing by outside authorities who allowed local people little voice in management strategies.

After the departure of the large-scale timber industry, many of the people who remained in the region turned to small farming. Wayne Blackwell, a resi-dent of the Ozarks, described the area as populated by people who had small patches of corn they took to larger neighboring communities for milling.[37] The ability to supply one's family with crops grown on your own land and processed in the community allowed many Ozarkers to hang on to a sense of self-sufficiency.

Woods-burning was a key element in many Ozarkers' strategy to suc-cessfully live in the hill country, and they refused to abandon it regardless of the state's wishes. Fire served as a basic tool for many subsistence farmers struggling to survive. Jack Toll, a resident of the Ozarks since the 1930s and a participant in the timber industry, explained why people burned the woods: "They burned it because it took the litter off, stimulated grass to grow, and a lot of the old timers said it killed all of the ticks."[38] Those who burned the hills did so out of a desire to shape the woods into a useful resource rather than to destroy a prominent element of their lives. Tom Martin, an Ozarker since his birth in Dent County in 1910, explained how his neighbors used fire: "They always burned out every spring. It didn't kill the timber then because there wasn't that many leaves. You let them leaves get knee deep and, lord it'll kill everything burned."[39] By annually employing fire, subsistence farmers in the most rugged areas of the Ozarks believed they could promote the growth of nutritive grass for their livestock as well as create and maintain an ideal place for harvesting game, wild plants, and wood for building and heating their homes. Woods-burning and the open range were closely inter-twined in their economic strategies and cultural attitudes towards the woods.

These subsistence farmers with small landholdings included the com-mons of the free range (fig. 20) in their economic strategies. Ab Dettwiler

[37] Wayne Blackwell and Icelene Blackwell, interview.
[38] Jack Toll, interview, 14.
[39] Tom Martin, interview, 13.

recalled, "We used to always burn every spring. You had to burn every spring, 'cause you see there wasn't no stock laws. People just turned their stock out, it was free range."[40] Roy Baugh, born along the Jacks Fork River in 1907, shared Dettwiler's assessment of fire and the open range. "We had to [burn], because it was open range and stuff. We didn't have no pastures built up, we had that open range, we couldn't afford it [pasture land]."[41] From the earliest European settlement in Missouri until the 1940s, and often later, woods-burning and the open range remained important in the culture, patterns of subsistence, and relationships with the woods of farmers in the rugged Ozarks.[42]

The issue of the open range engaged many people in debate, most prominently in discussions of the South. The economist Shawn Everett Kantor

Figure 20: John Vachon, "Goats on Ozark Mountain Farm" (Library of Congress, Prints and Photographs Division, FSA-OWI Collection [LC-USF34-061049-D DLC], black and white film negative, May 1940).

[40] Ab Dettwiler, interview, 6.

[41] Roy Baugh, interview, 28.

[42] For a supporting argument, see McWhiney and McDonald, "Celtic Origins of Southern Herding Practices."

provided an excellent analysis of the costs and benefits of enclosure throughout the South. On the history of conflicts over open range, however, his logic fell short when he contended that "the debate [over closing the range] was not a class or cultural conflict as some historians claim, but a battle between those who anticipated benefits from livestock enclosure and those who did not."[43] In the Courtois Hills, those who perceived the closing of the range as beneficial were of a decidedly different class and culture than the proponents of open range. To benefit from enclosure, an individual had to possess the means and desire to acquire and improve land for pasture, cultivation, and participation in market agriculture. These were not the traits of most residents of this region. Even after the close of the range, many in the Courtois Hills still would not embrace agriculture based on the market.

Fence laws were frequently debated in the rural United States as farming shifted from subsistence to market production. Steven Hahn argues that the campaign to close the range in the upcountry of Georgia was in part motivated by race, but was also a clash of cultural attitudes towards the market. The region's elite sought to abolish common grazing and hunting rights in favor of more manageable and profitable enclosures during the 1880s. Robert C. McMath Jr. notes that farmers on the Texas frontier, with a conscious reflection on the social and economic implications of enclosure on the lower classes in England, revolted violently against fence law advocates at the same time the issue was under debate in Georgia.[44] Despite differing levels of philosophical objection to the idea of a closed range, subsistence-oriented rural people across the United States refused to abandon common grazing rights.

Missourians who called for the enclosure of the range demonstrated a difference in cultural attitudes from Ozarkers who relied upon the commons. The state passed its first stock laws contemporaneously with similar nationwide movements in the 1870s, but these laws only closed the range in some areas and only on the basis of local option votes. Thomas T. Hathaway of St. Louis spoke for proponents of a closed range when he addressed his colleagues in the General Assembly regarding the option law: "It is a law acting

---

[43] Kantor, *Politics and Property Rights*, 14.

[44] Hahn, "Roots of Southern Populism," 331–76; and McMath, "Sandy Land and Hogs in the Timber," 216–21.

by counties only, whereas I would have it a general law, compulsorary [*sic*] in character, embracing every foot of domain in the borders of our State." Hathaway's statements reveal that he felt he knew what was best for everyone and every place in the state. This reformist attitude was at the center of many of the conflicts between those who chose to live in the Courtois Hills and the government. These hill folk resisted the efforts of proponents of the market economy like Hathaway, who claimed, "Speaking for the State of Missouri, nothing can be done to benefit the State so universally and to such an extent as the passage of a law which will compel the owners of stock to herd or confine their stock within secure limits." Hathaway assessed the costs and benefits of fence laws based on a comparison of investments versus profits in field crops and free ranged livestock.[45] This effort to create an economic analysis of the resources of the entirety of rural Missouri, despite local variations in environmental conditions, clearly demonstrates the cultural differences in outlook towards profit and resources that Kantor discounts.

Attitudes towards fire marked the most dramatic contrast between the beliefs of governmental agents and those who opposed them in the Ozarks. Record's assessment in 1908 marked the beginning of the government's approach to fire in the Ozarks. He argued that the state must create programs to educate the public against woods-burning because laws alone would not convince locals to discontinue the annual setting of fires.[46] The issue remained a top priority for governmental agents attempting to manage Ozark forests. L. W. Pickens, a resident of Camden County, reported to the U.S. Forest Service in 1920 regarding his displeasure with locals who burned the woods, "The woods is kept burning at all times except when it is too wet or until the whole country is burned over. At any time during the winter or early spring months when the leaves is dry the light from the forest fires can be seen at night in every direction." He added, "The result is we now have neither grass or timber."[47] Fire remained a key element of conflict as residents of the

[45] Hathaway, "Speech in favor of a stock law," 6–9.

[46] Record, "Missouri's Opportunities in Forestry," 4–5.

[47] L. W. Pickens to U.S. Forest Service, 22 January 1920, folder 65, Dunlap Papers; and von Schrenk, "Report of the Missouri Forestry Commission," sect. 48, p. 6. For more information on foresters' evolving attitudes towards fire, see Schiff, *Fire and Water.*

most rugged areas resisted the efforts of the government and other reformers who attempted to create conservation policies.

Concern over Forest Depletion

Despite the state's general failures, early conservation between 1908 and 1921 uncovered many of the issues that would be at the center of later efforts. In 1911, the federal government approved a bill proposed by John W. Weeks to create national forests in the eastern United States. Before passage of the Weeks Forest Purchase Act, Congress had restricted the establishment of federal forests to public domain lands, which were almost entirely in the West, and they had taken authority over those lands out of the president's hands in 1907. The Weeks Act created a new role for the federal government. Beginning in 1911, the United States could purchase forested or cutover land in the East to protect the watersheds of navigable waterways. But one component of the act stipulated that states had to pass enabling legislation to allow the federal government to purchase land within their boundaries, and this component proved fatal to the success of the act in Missouri.[48] Because Missouri refused to pass such legislation until the 1930s, the federal government would not enter the state under the auspices of the original Weeks Act.[49] This act, however, set the stage for the creation of a governmental presence in the Missouri woods.[50]

Unable to join the movement for national forests, Missouri's conservationists sought other ways to transfer land to government hands. In his annual report for 1917, State Game and Fish Commissioner Tim Birmingham noted,

> At the last session of the Legislature an act was passed requiring the Commissioner to set aside, out of the total receipts of the of the Department, a sum not less than 5 percent of the total receipts, for the purchase of a state park; the purpose of this act

[48] Robinson, *Forest Service*, 10–11.

[49] With the passage of the Clarke-McNary Act in 1924, the federal government added the authority to purchase lands for timber production to the original goal of watershed production; Robinson, *Forest Service*, 10–12, 146, 244.

[50] Callison, *Man and Wildlife*, 14–15; Folk, "Address by Joseph W. Folk," in Blanchard et al., *Proceeding of a Conference of Governors*, 158; and Mark J. Boesch, "Role of National Forests in Missouri," 2, in Forests and Forestry—Missouri, vertical file, SHS Ref. Libr.

is to create a fund to acquire a large, well-watered tract of land somewhere in the state particularly adapted to game and fish where the work of propagation and protection can be carried on under the most favorable conditions.[51]

This fund was completely inadequate to create a state park system, but it was an important and controversial step forward. Despite Birmingham's assertion that parks would be used to propagate game, sportsmen remained irate over the earmarking of funds away from fish and game for the establishment of parks. Sportsmen would eventually become frustrated with declining game populations and feel that the money spent on parks could be put to better use.[52]

The dire status of Missouri's forests continued to draw the attention of national leaders into the second decade of the century. In 1918 Raphael Zon, an employee of the U.S. Forest Service and future director of the Lake States Forest Experiment Station in Minnesota, relayed the results of his timber survey of Missouri to Frederick Dunlap, a forestry professor at the state university and future Missouri state forester. Zon found that only 14,000,000 acres of woodland remained among the state's 43,985,000 acres and that 8,919,000 of those forested acres were on farms and were subject to grazing. In addition to these problems, 95 percent of Missouri's remaining timber was composed of hardwoods that were less valuable to timbermen than the state's depleted pine.[53]

Even where timber remained in the Ozarks, much of it had already been cut over at least once. A former employee of the MLM, George T. Lee, noted in 1919, that "Ig [sic] has been the custom of the Missouri Lumber & Mining Company to occasionally sell small tracts of their timber lands to little sawmill operators in the above counties [Carter and Shannon], who manufacture the timber left on such tracts into Railroad Cross Ties and Switch Ties."[54] Lee, possibly the same man who represented Carter County in the General Assembly during the previous decade, pointed to a significant development. After the MLM left the region, many residents who stayed sought economic

[51] McCanse, *Annual Report of the State Game and Fish Commissioner*, 47, 53–55.

[52] Callison, *Man and Wildlife*, 15; Howard, "Missouri's Timber Supply"; and Boesch, "Role of National Forests in Missouri," 1, in Forests and Forestry—Missouri, vertical file, SHS Ref. Libr.

[53] Raphael Zon to Frederick Dunlap, 8 October 1918, folder 159, Dunlap Papers.

[54] Statement of George T. Lee, 30 September 1919, folder 6867, MLM Records.

independence by hacking ties from hardwoods on small, cutover parcels of land, generally in conjunction with subsistence farming. As economic conditions in the hills declined, many came to recognize tie-hacking as one of very few ways residents could still find employment.[55]

Missouri's first substantive efforts towards establishing an effective forest policy emerged when the timbermen who remained in the state determined that a cooperative relationship with the government was necessary to prevent further deterioration of profits. By the second decade of the twentieth century, the economic potential of the state's forests was dramatically impoverished. A handful of timber companies continued to work in the region, but generally at a small scale and mostly dedicated to the production of railroad ties and barrel staves from oak.

When the MLM pulled out of Grandin, the company sold off the town and much of its land, but not everything. The MLM maintained a presence in the town under the supervision of John Nathan Sparks, who had the title of assistant supervisor. Sparks's personal papers suggest that he served as the broker for the MLM's remaining lands in the Ozarks during the 1920s. J. N. Sparks, most likely the same man, had begun his employ with the MLM on at least one log drive in 1905.[56] Apparently the MLM's single remaining representative in Grandin, Sparks was brutally honest about the condition of the region. When E. A. Hurt wrote from Oklahoma in 1921 in search of work, Sparks replied, "The Smalley Company has stopped buying ties and I suppose will close out their business. Ties have fallen off about half."[57] In a letter that same year to a man from Standard, Louisiana (a community where MLM investors operated a mill), Sparks told I. C. Smith, "In reply to your letter of August 1st I will say that if you are in any deader place than Missouri is at present time you would not have the nerve or energy to try to leave. There is nothing being done here that a man can get into now that he could make a living at."[58] Sparks's correspondence reveals the difficulties faced by residents of the Courtois Hills and timber companies in the dreary years of the 1920s. The

[55] Robert Hargis and Corky Hargis, interview.

[56] J. B. White to C. C. Sheppard, 30 January 1905, folder 8, MLM Records.

[57] J. N. Sparks to E. A. Hurt, 18 January 1921, folder 16, Sparks Papers.

[58] J. N. Sparks to I. C. Smith, 4 August 1921, folder 19, Sparks Papers.

yellow pine was gone, the tie industry was declining, and no new industries were moving into the region. Individuals who could support themselves on small, rocky farms and the open range were able to subsist—barely.

The Missouri Forestry Association and State Forestry

Missouri's timbermen responded to the challenges they faced by organizing the Missouri Forestry Association (MFA) in 1921 to seek a rational forest policy and thereby maintain the viability of the industry. The organization, membership, funding, and goals of the MFA revealed its basis as an industrialists' association. The timbermen came together at a dinner sponsored by the Lumbermen's Exchange of St. Louis and the Tie and Timber Division of the St. Louis Chamber of Commerce. Six of the association's founding officers either owned, or were employed by, timber companies.[59] Frederick Dunlap, founding member and secretary of the MFA, admitted that the association owed a debt to the state's "lumber dealers and producers as well as bankers and wholesalers."[60] The association counted on its individual members—fifty-seven joined at the organizational meeting—to provide the bulk of its start-up money through dues of two dollars per member. Approximately three hundred dollars of the association's initial capitalization, however, was loaned by timber companies. The MFA also obtained free office space and clerical assistance in St. Louis from the National Association of Railway Tie Producers.[61]

The MFA emerged as part of an effort to maintain the state's forests for the timber industry. This set up a dual possibility for conflict in the Courtois Hills in particular. Several residents of the region had seized on the employment and wages of the MLM and affiliated companies and as a consequence harbored a deep distrust of the industry that had abandoned the region without any warning. Others in the region simply wanted to control the forests as they saw fit as part of their efforts to independently subsist. The MFA was troubled by the general unwillingness of residents of the most cutover sections to cooperate with forestry measures. Although some promoters of forest

---

[59] "The organization meeting of the Missouri Forestry ...," December 1921, folder 275, Dunlap Papers; and Missouri Forestry Association, Articles of Incorporation, 7 December 1921, folder 275, Dunlap Papers.

[60] Frederick Dunlap to Clinton G. Smith, 17 July 1922, folder 160, Dunlap Papers.

[61] "Report of the second annual meeting," 3 February 1922, folder 276, Dunlap Papers.

policy believed the rapid deforestation of Missouri since 1880 prepared people to accept forest management, many forestry professionals remained pes-
simistic. Hermann von Schrenk attributed Missouri's forestry problems to "a
back-woods farmer element in this State, with a more or less active politician
leading them who is against everything."[62] Foresters and woodland residents
continued to struggle for control throughout the 1920s, without a resolution.

By the early 1920s, many of Missouri's remaining timber companies
began to work through the MFA to encourage their colleagues to undertake
forestry programs. The association used trade meetings, direct mailings, and
demonstrations of forestry techniques to persuade timbermen that the application of scientific forestry was necessary for the survival of the industry.[63]
These efforts encouraged timbermen to move towards conservation practices,
and by 1923, Dunlap could report that ten-year cutting rotations on parcels
of 100,000 acres had begun to appear.[64] Once timbermen threw their support
behind the new association, the MFA had the economic and political influence to push for forestry policy and legislation.

Industrial leaders and professional foresters opposed the establishment of
national forests in Missouri, preferring instead to consolidate what support
existed for forestry in the hands of a single state agency headed by educated
forestry professionals. It is likely that industrialists within Missouri preferred
a state rather than a federal agency because it would be more susceptible to
their influence. Dunlap wrote to C. R. Tillotson of the U.S. Forest Service
in 1923, "My own opinion is that we should first make an attempt to solve
our forest problem through the agency of a State department rather than at
this time call in the Federal Forest Service."[65] William B. Greeley, chief of
the forest service from 1920 to 1928, agreed: "It would be distinctly prefer-
able not to press the idea of establishing a National Forest in the state." He
explained, "To do so would confuse the issue and quite possibly injure the

[62] Frederick Dunlap to Hermann von Schrenk, 16 January 1922, folder 166, Dunlap Papers; Report
of the "Forestry Division," 663; and Hermann von Schrenk to W. B. Greeley, 25 August 1922, folder 168,
Dunlap Papers.

[63] Frederick Dunlap to Hermann von Schrenk, 30 December 1921, folder 165; and Hermann von
Schrenk to [1500 lumbermen], 17 February 1923, folder 169, both items in Dunlap Papers.

[64] Frederick Dunlap to C. R. Tillotson, 30 June 1923, folder 161, Dunlap Papers.

[65] Frederick Dunlap to C. R. Tillotson, 20 January 1922, folder 159, Dunlap Papers.

chances of securing legislation for the establishment of a State Forestry Board, which is now before the legislature. ... The first thing you need in Missouri is a State agency of your own which can study all of these questions and formulate a program for the best solution."[66] The leaders of both the state and national forestry movements agreed that trained individuals with a stake in the future of the forests needed to gain control of Missouri's resources.

The creation of an official state forestry agency occupied much of the association's efforts. In 1923, MFA agents wrote a bill designed to create a state forestry agency and planned their winter and spring activities around the bill. When the General Assembly debated the MFA's bill, as Senate Bill 88 and House Bill 200, Hermann von Schrenck, president of the MFA, sent mailings to 1,500 lumbermen in an effort to gain support for the bill and membership in the association.[67] By March, the General Assembly had decided against the measure. Von Schrenk responded by immediately beginning a campaign for a similar bill for the following year. Despite the association's efforts, the legislature rejected the proposed forestry department again in 1924.[68] Undaunted, the timbermen pressed on.

In order to gain the greatest possible success, the MFA undertook vigorous efforts to broaden its membership beyond its original foundation—industrialists. Dunlap and von Schrenk sought to gain support from the Missouri Horticultural Society, the Missouri Federation of Women's Clubs, and sportsmen's organizations.[69] The association also sent direct mailings, authored newspaper releases, and published at least a few issues of a magazine, *The Conservation Advocate.*[70] But the association never extended this membership drive to include

---

[66] W. B. Greeley to Charles F. Hatfield, 10 February 1923, folder 163, Dunlap Papers.

[67] Hermann von Schrenk to [1,500 lumbermen], 17 February 1923, folder 169, Dunlap Papers.

[68] Voluminous correspondence surrounds the MFA's efforts to establish a forestry department in 1923 and 1924. For a representative sampling, see Frederick Dunlap to "All annual members [of the MFA]," 8 February 1923, folder 276; Hermann von Schrenk to Frederick Dunlap, 6 March 1923, folder 169; "Minutes of council meeting," 13 November 1924, folder 276; and *Conservation Advocate* no. 2 (September 1925): 3–4, folder 1, all items in Dunlap Papers.

[69] Hermann von Schrenk to Frederick Dunlap, 2 February 1923, folder 169; and Frederick Dunlap to "The sportsmen of Missouri," 13 November 1924, folder 275, both in Dunlap Papers. Unfortunately, there is no indication of success or failure in broadening the association's support base.

[70] Frederick Dunlap to Hermann von Schrenk, 19 November 1921, folder 164; F. Dunlap to Hermann von Schrenck, 22 December 1921, folder 165; F. Dunlap to Hermann von Schrenck, 17 October 1921, folder 164; and *Conservation Advocate* no. 2 (September 1925), folder 1, all items in Dunlap Papers. The *Conservation Advocate* ran for an indeterminate number of issues and never declared its subscription

the families living on small farms among the forests in question (generally in the Ozarks), a crucial oversight common to early conservationists.

The association pursued two primary goals, both with the same ultimate purpose: a state forestry program and the conservation of forests for industrial use. The purpose of the MFA, as stated on the association's letterhead, was "to advance the public understanding of the importance of timber crops, so that due provision will be made for insuring forests so maintained and cared for as to furnish a supply of timber for future needs."[71] The association attempted to achieve its goals by preventing fire, reestablishing woodlands, and educating Missourians in forestry. These activities would continue to dominate the activities of subsequent forestry agencies in the state.

In 1925, the General Assembly finally agreed to provide for a state forester within the Board of Agriculture. But in late April, Dunlap had the duty of passing bad news along to an MFA colleague: "Governor Baker indicates that he will veto the forestry bill enacted by the General Assembly this winter due to lack of funds to make it effective."[72] Approximately two weeks later, however, Dunlap noted that "Governor Baker has signed our forestry bill and it now becomes law at midnight July 9, next."[73] It is unclear what caused the governor to change his mind. The most logical explanation, however, lies in funding.

Developments at the federal level may have influenced the state to finally allocate funds to forestry. In 1924, the federal government passed the Clarke-McNary Act to create a means of cooperating with states in fire prevention. By setting aside money for forestry and instituting a fire protection program, however rudimentary, Missouri would become eligible for funds from the federal government. The actions of Missouri's political leaders suggest that they were only willing to push for conservation when the state government would bear a disproportionately small share of the cost.[74]

numbers.

[71] Frederick Dunlap, "To the Sportsmen of Missouri," 13 November 1924, folder 275; and *Conservation Advocate* no. 2 (September 1925): 2, folder 1, both items in Dunlap Papers.

[72] Frederick Dunlap to Foster Schroeder, 22 April 1925, folder 148, Dunlap Papers.

[73] Frederick Dunlap to J. G. Peters, 5 May 1925, folder 163, Dunlap Papers.

[74] Boesch, "Role of National Forests," 2, in Forests and Forestry—Missouri, vertical file, SHS Ref Libr.; "Minutes of council meeting," 13 November 1924, folder 276, Dunlap Papers; and "New Forestry Division," 664.

In August 1925, the Missouri State Board of Agriculture elected Frederick Dunlap as the first state forester and determined that he would receive a salary of $3,000. The bill that created the new forestry division within the Board of Agriculture stated that the MFA would pay Dunlap's salary. Furthermore, the University of Missouri Agricultural Extension Service and the U.S. Department of Agriculture would cooperate to contribute the money to cover Dunlap's expenses while he conducted fieldwork and promoted the planting of "farm timber patches." The State of Missouri created a state office for forestry without appropriating a dime.[75] The result was a state forester who was essentially paid by the timber industry. Without the association's stipend, Missouri would not have been eligible for federal money, and the state was unwilling to establish a forestry program without significant federal support. Governor Sam Baker was willing to sign the bill once the salary and operating expenses for the new division were covered.

The duties of the state forester proved too numerous for a single individual, which led to the employment of Paul Dunn as the state's only district forester. He worked out of an office in Ellington, in Reynolds County on the edge of the Courtois Hills. Dunn described his role: "My assignment was to carry out a program with the school systems and timber companies in what we called fire protection education, introducing into the school system the need for prevention and control of fire." Persuading residents of the area to abandon woods-burning dominated Dunn's efforts. He later assessed the program: "It was reasonably successful. However, most of the people in the area didn't consider the woods burning harmful."[76] This first incarnation of forest conservation in Missouri was designed to target the minds of those residing in or near the Ozark woods as the key to ensuring the forest's future. Dunlap and Dunn believed they could end woods-burning by educating the next generation to discontinue the practice.

During the same years that the MFA was seeking to establish a state forestry office in Missouri, the state finally began to acquire some state parks. The 5 percent diversion from hunting and fishing licenses proved insufficient, so in 1923 the legislature increased the amount of money set aside from license sales

---

[75] "New Forestry Division," 823.
[76] Dunn, "St. Regis Paper Company," interview, 4–5.

to 25 percent, providing the necessary funds for the creation of state parks. By 1925, Keith McCanse, the game and fish commissioner, was able to report to Governor Baker, "Our system now comprises eight state parks with a total area of 23,224 acres." He identified the largest parks in the system as Salem State Park in Dent County (12,868 acres), Ellington State Park in Reynolds County (4,920 acres), and Big Spring State Park in Carter County (4,258 acres), which combined to account for the majority of the system. The next largest park was Bennett Spring with a mere 574 acres. McCanse also noted that Alley Spring State Park with 427 acres and Round Spring with another 75 acres were both in Shannon County.[77] Missouri chose to locate the beginnings of its state park system among the dramatic hills, bluffs, rivers, and forests of the Courtois Hills and adjacent lands. This region, however, was also home to some determined resistance to governmental control of resources.

Deforestation in Missouri reached its most severe levels during the first years of the twentieth century, then stabilized by the end of the second decade. In 1925, Dunlap reported that forests covered approximately 40 percent of the state, or roughly eighteen million acres. Although this number was much smaller than Dunlap desired, he discovered a positive trend. In the previous five years, the number of acres converted from woodlands to agricultural land had declined in most Missouri counties. Dunlap also believed that fewer than two million acres of additional forestlands in the state would fall to agriculture. He felt that all of the land with agricultural potential had been taken up and the remaining lands would retain their forests.[78] This decrease in land cleared for agriculture coincided with the postwar decline in the fortunes of farmers throughout the state and the nation.

Dunlap and other leaders vigorously called for reforestation in Missouri to ensure a future resource for the timber industry. As state forester, he proclaimed, "There is between fifteen and sixteen million acres of land in Missouri that is making no adequate contribution to the prosperity of the community in which it lies. Thirty-five percent of the state is sunning itself to no useful purpose."[79] Based on his statement that 40 percent of Missouri

[77] McCanse, *Annual Report of the State Game and Fish Commissioner*, 47, 53–55.
[78] Dunlap, "Missouri's Development Through Forestry," 958–59.
[79] Dunlap, "Missouri's Development Through Forestry," 958.

was forested, it seems likely that Dunlap considered much of the state's forest-land in need of management before it would become truly productive. Forest Service Chief William B. Greeley also believed that the fate of Missouri's forests was in jeopardy: "The tide of forest depletion has traveled west and it has not confronted you [Missouri] as it has the eastern sections. It cannot be expected that the public here will be as active as in the East, but it will develop the same way." Greeley argued that Missouri would not establish an effective forestry program until deforestation posed an obvious threat to the economy and aesthetics of the state.[80] The MFA, however, attempted to prove Greeley wrong by pushing for rational management of forests before its members lost the resources they depended on for their income.

Throughout the 1920s, forest policy remained under the influence of tim-bermen. The MFA interpreted "farm timber" as woodlots that would ensure a source of timber well into the future. As the primary source of funding for state forestry through 1928, the association had at least some opportunity to influence the direction of state policy. Dunlap, accordingly, encouraged farmers to devote a greater percentage of their land to woodlots despite the resistance he faced from the Missouri Farm Bureau. The elimination of woodland grazing and the annual burning of forests were such key issues for forest policy that Dunlap was willing to risk alienating the powerful Farm Bureau if he could improve the state's forest resources.[81] The state forester's goals of "PREVENTION OF WILDFIRE and PLANTING FARM TIM-BER" (emphasis in original) reflected the desires of industrialists.[82] Although he certainly considered the value of woodlots for timber production, Dunlap performed much of his work in northern Missouri where woodlots could also provide much-needed protection from erosion.

As the 1920s drew to a close, the health of Missouri's timberlands and the forest industry continued to concern Dunlap. He estimated that the state used over 140 million board feet of softwoods in 1928, but the state's forests pro-duced less than 39 million board feet. The estimated figures for hardwoods were

[80] "Dr. H. von Schrenk Elected President of Missouri Forestry Body," *St. Louis Globe-Democrat* (ca. 1921), folder 276, Dunlap Papers.

[81] Frederick Dunlap to J. G. Peters, 21 February 1925, folder 163, Dunlap Papers; and Dunlap, "Missouri's Development Through Forestry," 959.

[82] Dunlap, "What the Forestry Department Is Doing," 1930, folder 274, Dunlap Papers.

slightly better at just over 135 million board feet used and about 102 million board feet produced. Dunlap explained the impact of this industrial harvest on the forests of the Ozarks: "When the pine timber was logged off and the land burned over the pine had no chance to replace itself but its place was taken by the oaks, and too often by the blackjack oak, which represents the most worthless form of forest growth that we find in Missouri." The state forester's analysis was particularly significant because he also argued that in 1928 oak accounted for roughly 44 percent of all lumber sawed in Missouri.[83] Missouri's shortleaf pine was essentially gone, leaving the state's timber industry dependent on the less valuable oaks.

Industry Steps Away from Conservation

The MFA retreated from the public arena after 1928, though there are indications that the association may have survived in some form until 1937. Coincident with the apparent collapse of the association, the General Assembly appropriated funds to support Frederick Dunlap's work as state forester in 1929.[84] It is unclear whether the disappearance of the timbermen's funds led to the state's picking up the costs of the office or if the association melted away because it lost its defining rationale for existence once the state was willing to pay the tab for conservation. Although this appropriation was small and would prove short-lived, just a single biennium, it was a key event, as the state finally agreed to fund a program of forest conservation.

With the provision of money directly from the state, Dunlap began to concentrate more time on farm-forestry projects, but forest conservation in Missouri remained devoted to industrial timber production. When the Central States Forestry Congress convened in December 1930, Missouri sent representatives from five corporations, one of which was partially owned by a future governor of the state. Other than Missouri, Tennessee and Pennsylvania were the only states to have even one spokesperson from a private company. The other participating states sent representatives from state universities and conservation agencies.[85] Dunlap, however, determined that in

[83] Dunlap, "Flora," 125–27.

[84] "Report of the Forestry Division," *State of Mo.: Official Manual . . . Nineteen Twenty-Nine and Nineteen Thirty,* 818.

[85] Central States Forestry Congress Program, 3–5 December 1930, p. 2, folder 273, Dunlap Papers.

1930 he spent 43 percent of his time on nursery work and the majority of the remainder advising private landowners, mostly farmers, but he also worked with some mill owners.[86] A large portion of these duties kept Dunlap in northern and central Missouri; Paul Dunn held most of the responsibility for programs in the Ozarks.

Missouri's foresters still emphasized the prevention and fighting of fires in their interactions with the public. Dunlap theorized that fire was the most significant problem Missouri's forests faced, partly because the public did not realize the damage such conflagrations caused.[87] Without proper protection from fire, Dunlap feared, Missouri's trees would lose their resistance to the growth of fungus that led to rotten centers in timber.[88] The forester stated, "Our fires will be brought under control when these people [rural Missourians] know how to control them and in its work for the control of wildfire this Department is exercising no police power—it has none—but it is organizing local communities for the control of their own fire."[89] Dunlap and Dunn relied on programs of education to convey their attitude towards the natural world to Ozarkers. Once again, outsiders with the authority to call for changes in the woodlands held a set of values that were different from those of most subsistence-oriented rural Missourians concerning forest resources.

Efforts to prevent forest fires in the Missouri Ozarks went beyond the creation of fire lines and the construction of fire towers. Because of the agency's limited manpower, foresters ultimately relied on gaining the support of locals so they would be more amenable to providing governmental officials with assistance. By demonstrating "proper" forestry throughout rural Missouri and convincing farmers to plant trees, Dunlap hoped to convince the public that fires destroyed the very forests they painstakingly planted and maintained.[90] By 1930, foresters had gained a small measure of success in persuading farmers that forest fires created more damage than revitalization in the woods.

[86] "Distribution of time of…," 1930, folder 273, Dunlap Papers.

[87] "Report of the Forestry Division," *State of Mo.: Official Manual… Nineteen Twenty-Nine and Nineteen Thirty*, 818.

[88] Dunlap, "Missouri's Development Through Forestry," 959.

[89] Dunlap, "What the Forestry Department Is Doing," (1930), 2, folder 274, Dunlap Papers.

[90] "Report of the Forestry Division," *State of Mo.: Official Manual… Nineteen Twenty-Nine and Nineteen Thirty*, 818; and Dunlap, "What the Forestry Department Is Doing," 1930, folder 274, Dunlap Papers.

On 1 June 1931, Missouri reconsidered its funding for state-sponsored forest conservation and determined that the results did not warrant continued appropriations. The General Assembly concluded that it could no longer pay the salary of state and district foresters.[91] This decision undoubtedly bore some relation to the onset of the Great Depression. The state and district foresters responded to Missouri's penuriousness by resigning in 1931.[92] Charles Callison argues that Dunlap resigned in part because he felt it was impossible to get Ozarkers to abandon woods-burning.[93] The failure of the state to renew the appropriation left Missouri without any state forestry program whatsoever.

Although Dunn and Dunlap both left the state, Dunlap continued to carry on correspondence with individuals in Missouri devoted to the establishment of state forestry. Dunn moved on to several appointments, including teaching at Utah Agricultural College, serving as that state's head forester and fire warden, and assisting in the establishment of state forestry in Chile.[94] Both remained devoted to forest conservation throughout their careers.

The MFA, Dunlap, and Dunn all worked to solidify state-sponsored forest conservation in Missouri, but they could not gather the necessary public support. For several years after the state and district foresters resigned, Missouri made no significant progress in gaining control of the Ozark forests. As conservation issues continued to draw significant debate, the importance of the hill country formerly dominated by the MLM increasingly sat at the forefront of the discussion. During the Great Depression and the New Deal of the 1930s, however, Missouri would witness a series of social and economic changes that would allow for a new beginning in conservation in the Courtois Hills, Ozarks, and the state as a whole.

---

[91] Callison, *Man and Wildlife*, 96.

[92] "Report of the Forestry Division," *State of Mo.: Official Manual… Nineteen Thirty-One and Nineteen Thirty-Two*, 626.

[93] Callison, *Man and Wildlife*, 96.

[94] Keefe, *First 50 Years*, 202; "Report of the Forestry Division," *State of Mo.: Official Manual… Nineteen Thirty-One and Nineteen Thirty-Two*, 626; and Paul M. Dunn, interview.

Chapter 5

A Governmental Foothold, 1931 to 1946

In the 1930s and 1940s, residents of the most rugged portions of the Missouri Ozarks faced a new set of circumstances in their attempts to create survival strategies in their beloved hill country. In the preceding two decades, local residents had considered the potential entrance of government into the Courtois Hills to pose more negative than positive possibilities. Industrialists of the same period were suspicious of any governmental efforts at conservation they could not control. During the 1930s and 1940s, the situation changed somewhat as governmental agents successfully gained more control over forest policy in Missouri.[1] Some of this success was based on the ability of the state and federal governments to garner support among Ozarkers, but most of it was due to the federal government's willingness to assist the state in a time of economic crisis, the increasing interest in conservation among Missourians in general, and the efforts of large timber companies to manipulate their relationship with governmental conservation, whether to divest themselves of cutover land or to increase their levels of production.

The Formation of National Forests

Missouri made a halfhearted attempt to introduce a governmental presence

[1] For the best two studies of the growth of governmental involvement in forest policy in Missouri during the 1930s and 1940s, see Callison, *Man and Wildlife*; and Keefe, *First 50 Years*.

into the state when it passed a key piece of legislation in 1929. This action followed the federal government's passage of the Clarke-McNary Act of 1924, which expanded the powers the Weeks Act granted to Washington. The Weeks Act provided the federal government with the authority to purchase land to protect the watersheds of navigable waterways, but not for other purposes. After the federal government passed the Clarke-McNary Act, Washington gained the authority to purchase land for timber management, in addition to its existing authority of providing matching funds for reforestation and fire protection.[2] With this opportunity in mind, in 1929 the Missouri General Assembly finally passed enabling legislation to allow the U.S. Forest Service to purchase land in the state. The legislature undermined this action by restricting federal ownership to a maximum of 2,000 acres in any county, effectively preventing the Forest Service from establishing purchase units in Missouri and for all practical purposes negating the enabling act.[3]

Between 1931 and 1936, Missourians began to show more interest in the fate of the state's forests. Forest coverage remained between 35 and 40 percent of the state, but Missourians began to recognize some emerging problems. Within weeks of Frederick Dunlap's resignation from his position as state forester and the subsequent collapse of state forestry in 1931, the National Forest Reserve Association of Crawford, Dent, Iron, Reynolds, and Washington Counties formed "to secure the establishment of a national forest consisting of not less than 100,000 acres of land in the counties named."[4] These five Ozark counties provided the membership of this association from among the prominent citizens of the region's towns who were concerned with the poor quality of Missouri's forests.[5] The composition of this association reflects the diversity of opinion in the Ozarks. There was a sentiment in favor of conservation in some areas, though not of any consequence in most of the Courtois Hills area.

[2] Robinson, *Forest Service*, 10, 12, 146, 244.

[3] Keefe, *First 50 Years*, 202–3; and Stevens, *A Homeland and A Hinterland*, 196–97.

[4] "Five Counties Asking for National Forest," Salem *Post,* 22 June 1931, in *Missouri National Forests Association Book,* vol. 1, C1175, WHMC–Columbia.

[5] Robert Good to Hon. Guy B. Park, 21 June 1933, in *Missouri National Forests Association Book,* vol. 2, C1175, WHMC–Columbia.

The Missouri National Forests Association, a group that formed in September 1933 when the above association merged with a similar group from some neighboring counties, made its case by quoting figures supplied by the American Tree Association of Washington, DC.[6] They claimed that in 1933 Missouri only had 100,000 acres of "virgin" timber remaining and that the nearly three million acres of forestlands in the hands of timber companies contained nothing but second-growth timber.[7] Partly because of the declining quality of the state's forests, it was estimated that Missouri only produced 24 percent of the forest products it consumed in the early 1930s. The Missouri National Forests Association claimed that with management, however, the state could produce 825 million board feet of timber annually and easily meet its estimated need of 785 million board feet. Those Missourians who supported the creation of a forestry program argued that present conditions were unacceptable, but not irreversible, and national forests would be a good start towards improving the timberlands.[8]

Despite Missouri's environmental problems, many conservation-minded individuals remained optimistic. Missouri's conservationists expected the state's forests to improve significantly in the coming years. Ruth ford H. Westveld, a forester with the U.S. Forest Service, reported to the Missouri National Forests Association that Missouri's forests were regenerating well and that the state had great potential to regain its importance in the national timber industry.[9] Foresters such as Westveld remained optimistic that Missouri's forests had passed their nadir and would return to productivity. Foresters also argued that the state's geographical proximity to the nation's treeless plains meant Missouri could benefit dramatically from forest management because the state's timber producers would profit from a long-term relationship with the nearby market.[10]

---

[6] "Forestry Groups Organize New Association," Salem *Post,* 7 September 1933, in *Missouri National Forests Association Book,* vol. 1, C1175, WHMC–Columbia.

[7] "The Forestry Situation in the Central States," in *Missouri National Forests Association Book,* vol. 2, WHMC–Columbia.

[8] Dean R. W. Selvidge, "The Public Works Program and Reforestation in Missouri," unidentified newspaper clipping in *Missouri National Forests Association Book,* vol. 2, p. 18, WHMC–Columbia.

[9] Ruthford H. Westveld, untitled document, 20 April, 1933, in *Missouri National Forests Association Book,* vol. 2, pp. 1–2, WHMC–Columbia.

[10] Westveld, *Applied Silviculture,* 211, 216.

Individuals and associations concerned about the future of the state's forests considered governmental assistance a necessary component of any recovery. The Rolla *New Era* editorialized, "Missouri is faced with the prospect of
having upon its hands soon large areas of land that persistently refuse to yield
an appreciable tax revenue. State ownership and reforestation of such lands
has been the answer to this situation in other states. Missouri apparently must
give some consideration to the problem of establishing a policy with regard to
such lands."[11] This call for a state presence in the forests came from a newspaper well within the Ozark region. Despite Missouri's slow progress in forest
conservation, there remained a segment of the population, even within the
Ozarks, committed to the creation of governmental forest policies.

Individuals promoting the conservation of fish, game, and forests in Missouri faced many challenges during the first half of the 1930s. One challenge
was the intermittent support by officials charged with executing state policies.
The severe economic distress the Missouri Ozarks suffered in the first years of
the 1930s created a severe condition recognized by state game and fish commissioner John H. Ross. In his annual report for 1932, Ross stated,

> The depression brought a new phase of trouble to the enforce-
> ment division. Securing wild game and fish for needed meat
> by unemployed people has grown the past two years and for
> the past year has been seriously hindering enforcement. Many
> hundreds of unlicensed hunters who have been apprehended
> by wardens the past year would frankly admit they were not
> able to buy a license or pay a fine and would request that the
> warden take them to jail. Many justices of the peace and pros-
> ecuting attorneys refuse to file cases now where it is shown that
> the families are without work.[12]

The situation was dire for Ozarkers. In this economic climate, state officials
recognized that they could not carry out conservation policies that deprived

[11] "Land Utilization Program in Missouri Hindered by Restriction of Counties," Rolla *New Era*, 13
October 1933, in *Missouri National Forests Association Book*, vol. 1, WHMC–Columbia.
[12] Ross, *Annual Report, 1932*, 26.

rural Missourians of access to resources.

The Great Depression was a particularly difficult time in the Missouri Ozarks. As the economy collapsed throughout the state's cities, impoverished Missourians moved to the cutover lands of the Ozarks in hopes of farming to support their families. With little soil and land too rocky for productive agriculture throughout the rugged portions of the Ozarks, newcomers found a difficult situation (figs. 21 and 22). The influx of new settlers also kept the population density at a level well above what the land could support under the earlier practices of woods-burning and open-range grazing.

In the early 1930s, Missourians interested in forest conservation increasingly turned to the federal government to protect timber supplies. Despite the actions of the Missouri National Forest Association and other concerned citizens, the federal government created no national forests in Missouri until the state increased the acreage limit from its 1929 allowance of 2,000 to

Figure 21: John Vachon, "Rocky Land of Ozark Mountain Farmer, Missouri," May 1940 (Library of Congress, Prints and Photographs Division, FSA-OWI Collection [LC-USF34-061046-D DLC], black and white film negative, May 1940).

Figure 22: "Planting Corn" (Center for Ozark Studies Collection, series 21, Photographs, folder 35, p. 13. Special Collections and Archives, Missouri State University, Springfield).

25,000 acres per county in 1933, at a time when New Deal funds made possible the federal purchase and development of forestlands.[13] Under the new enabling act, the U.S. Forest Service laid out purchase units at the corners of counties to create contiguous forest blocks of at least 100,000 acres, the minimum size it deemed cost-effective to manage.

Many Missourians, including D. L. Bales, a resident of Eminence, waged a continuous campaign opposing federal ownership of Ozark forests. As a state senator, Bales had the opportunity to lead the fight against the expansion of the Forest Service's national forests in the lands he represented. In 1931, he wrote to J. N. Sparks, the land broker for the MLM, "I have yours of the 25th inst. in regard to increasing the number of acres of land which the Federal government may acquire in Missouri, for park purposes, and would like to call

[13] Stevens, *A Homeland and A Hinterland*, 196–97.

your attention to the effects of such a bill on such counties as Carter and Shannon." Bales did not make the distinction between national parks and forests as he opposed the loosening of acreage restrictions. He continued,

> You realize that these counties can now barely maintain their county government, and we can easily anticipate what the result would be if $1/3$ or $1/2$ of the taxable wealth of the county were removed from the tax books, the lands being acquired by the Federal government. National Parks are all right where the lands are not suited for home-making purposes and are not already occupied for such purposes, but when we pass an act, permitting the Federal Government to come into our section, confiscating homes by condemnation, it smacks too much of the policy that England for many years pursued in regards to Ireland.[14]

Although his rhetoric was clearly designed to excite the concerns of locals, Bales touched on key points. Many residents of the Courtois Hills feared the loss of their independence to a powerful federal government and were aware that their local governments could not sustain further losses of tax revenue.

The arrival of a federal presence in the Ozarks was a controversial issue throughout the region. Supporters argued, "The proposal [to establish national forests] may without hesitancy be said to satisfy the wishes of the more influential residents of the entire eastern Ozark areas."[15] This was not the only opinion on federal forests. A year later when expansion of the extant national forests was under debate, an opponent argued that "the people within the area are not pushing the matter but that it is the big interests wanting to unload cut-over land."[16] The federal government relied on a powerful cadre

[14] D. L. Bales to J. N. Sparks, 28 February 1931, folder 30, Sparks Papers.

[15] Dean R. W. Selvidge, "The Public Works Program and Reforestation in Missouri, Appendix I," in "Suggested Projects Submitted by the Public Works Committee to the Missouri Relief and Reconstruction Commission," 27 June 1933, in *Missouri National Forests Association Book*, vol. 2, WHMC–Columbia.

[16] Sam T. Rollins to Robert Good, 20 October 1933, in *Missouri National Forests Association Book*, vol. 2, WHMC–Columbia. The two men were discussing the efforts of Senator Bales to prevent the relaxation of acreage restrictions on national forests.

of supporters in the region, such as the MLM, but it fought the attitudes of many who feared an increased governmental presence.

One of the ways the federal government was able to overcome local resistance and move into the Ozarks was through the Civilian Conservation Corps. The CCC entered Missouri in 1933 and immediately made a significant impact. The corps established camps for forestry work, soil conservation projects, and to improve state parks. The state hosted approximately forty camps, four of which were in Carter County. Dent was the only other county in the state to host as many as three camps.[17] CCC workers at Big Spring State Park in Carter County constructed over twelve miles of roads, a series of buildings throughout the park, nature trails, a flood control system, and installed a water pump and several telephone lines.[18] These camps provided the federal government an opportunity to establish positive relationships with Ozarkers who needed jobs.

Missouri's conservationists recognized the potential benefits of a strong CCC presence in the state. Game and fish commissioner Wilbur C. Buford gushed with enthusiasm in his report for 1933: "Since last June, Missouri's system of State parks has undergone a most remarkable transformation, made possible through the work of the Civilian Conservation Corps in co-operation with the State Game & Fish Department.... The magnitude and scope of this development is indeed amazing."[19] The cooperation between the CCC and the Game and Fish Commission demonstrated the potential for future successful relationships between federal and state conservation agencies.

The potential for stable employment through the federal government was one of the features that attracted Missourians to the idea of federal conservation. According to the Rolla *Herald*, the CCC had employed 310,000 men throughout the nation by August 1933.[20] Missouri's leaders recognized this agency as a potential windfall and wanted to participate. Buford argued that as of 1934 the "United States government has spent $690,000 in developing Missouri Parks, and before the U.S. Department of the Interior with-

[17] Keefe, *First 50 Years*, 204.

[18] Stevens, *A Homeland and A Hinterland*, 183–90.

[19] Buford, *Annual Report of the State Game and Fish Commissioner... 1933*, 6.

[20] "A Twenty Year Forest Program," Rolla *Herald*, 17 August 1933, in *Missouri National Forests Association Book*, vol. 1, WHMC–Columbia.

draws the CCC camps from these areas more than $1,000,000 will have been spent."[21] By late 1935, the U.S. Forest Service employed men at twenty-two separate camps in the Ozark region, where Big Spring State Park, in the heart of Carter County, emerged as one of the state's largest camps.[22]

The character of this employment proved more beneficial to residents of the Ozarks than one might expect. Most historians posit that the CCC, among its other goals, intended to employ out-of-work young men from the nation's cities in order to take them out of a poverty-stricken and crime-inducing environment and place them in a context of discipline and productive labor. According to the director of the CCC, sixty out of every one hundred enrollees to the federal program were actually from rural areas.[23] Galen Pike, the forest supervisor stationed in Springfield, MO, described an especially important component of the CCC in the Ozarks. He noted that even when the number of enrollees at CCC camps in the region declined, the number of LEMs (local experienced men, chosen for their knowledge of the region and the woods and not subject to most CCC regulations) held steady.[24] Local residents undoubtedly came to view the federal government in a more positive light as a result of the efforts of the CCC to open positions for local men and the agency's respect for their knowledge.

The employees of the CCC gave the federal government a personal face in the region for Ozarkers to interact with and provided local residents with many benefits. The CCC created jobs, improved forests and parks, and offered such social activities as baseball games, boxing matches, and dances.[25] The Leaders Improvement Club of CCC camp 3737 (located near Lynchburg, MO, at some remove from the Courtois Hills, but still in the Ozarks) hosted several events for the community during its tenure. In 1936, the group's "Camp Carnival" drew over five hundred people to the camp to engage in Halloween festivities.[26] Ozarkers living near the camps seemed to have wholeheartedly seized upon the

[21] Buford, *Annual Report of the State Game and Fish Commissioner... 1933*, 6.

[22] Kelleter, "The Forest Service in Missouri," speech notes, 25 November 1935, p. 2, folder 2, Kelleter Speeches; and Buford, *Annual Report of the State Game and Fish Commissioner... 1935*, 45.

[23] U.S. Federal Security Agency, *Final Report of the Director of the Civilian Conservation*, 112.

[24] Galen Pike, interview, 2, 5.

[25] Ibid., 8.

[26] Unidentified newspaper clipping, 1936, CCC Camp No. 3737 Papers.

services provided and become much more favorably disposed to governmental involvement as a result. Corky Hargis noted that other federal agencies, the Works Progress Administration in particular, also provided substantial help in the region. She recalled the agency's providing sewing machines and helping local residents make new mattresses.[27]

The CCC performed important duties as a relief organization in the region. In 1935, Acting Forest Ranger Dudley W. Gilmore asked the MLM's still-very-active land broker John Sparks to join him for a tour of a CCC camp near Winona, in Shannon County, as part of a publicity campaign. Gilmore promised a demonstration of some of the camp's work, including "truck trail constructions, low water crossing constructions, timber stand improvement, lookout tower operation, roadside hazard removal, and truck trail surfacing."[28] Ferrel Dablemont recalled the role of the CCC in the Ozarks as a "godsend" for the people of the region.[29] The CCC employed locals, provided recreational opportunities, and improved the region's forests, thereby enhancing the image of government-sponsored conservation. According to Kaufman, the CCC and the U.S. Forest Service offered Ozarkers much-needed personal contact with federal employees and the hope of work in construction and firefighting endeavors.[30]

While the federal government was establishing CCC camps and pursuing national forests in Missouri, the once-mighty MLM was still desperately trying to sell large amounts of cutover land in the Ozarks. The company viewed the creation of national forests as an opportunity to unload land that no one else would buy. In a letter of 8 October 1934, Leslie S. Bean, the U.S. Forest Service's Forest Supervisor at Rolla, wrote to J. N. Sparks, "I have been informed that the National Forest Reservation Commission will meet between October 22 and 27." Bean explained that because this would be the last meeting of the year and the committee was responsible for approving all purchases, "It will be necessary to have the options in this office by October 15."[31] In an obvious rush to take advantage of this opportunity, Sparks

---

[27] Robert Hargis and Corky Hargis, interview.
[28] Dudley W. Gilmore to J. N. Sparks, 24 September 1935, folder 271, Sparks Papers.
[29] Ferrel Dablemont, interview.
[30] Kaufman, "Social Factors," 71–73.
[31] Leslie S. Bean to J. N. Sparks, 8 October 1934, folder 256, Sparks Papers.

informed R. B. White (John Barber White's son and acting vice president of the MLM), who sent off a letter and the option forms to sell MLM lands to the federal government the very next day: "You will find enclosed, duly executed on behalf of this Company, purchase option in triplicate to the United States Department of Agriculture, covering 3,127.31 acres in Carter and Ripley Counties."[32] Although individuals such as Bales, who represented Ozarkers, opposed the creation of federal forests, the MLM continued to push for what it saw as a solution to its problem of cutover lands. For the MLM, these cutover lands were little other than an economic burden.

The MLM's support for national forests in Missouri proved significant. The company's influence in the Ozarks long after it had "cut out and got out" is suggested by R. B. White's comment to Sparks: "I have yours of October 1st and note that Mr. Bales has withdrawn and that Mr. Searcy has been named State Senator from his district by the Democratic party." White then told Sparks, "It looks like you have done some good work down there in behalf of Mr. Searcy. At your convenience I wish you would write me what the recent reforestation program is that Searcy has promised to support."[33] Through a more or less active campaign, Sparks contributed to the replacement of the leading local opponent of national forests with a man who favored forestry and conservation, especially federal land purchases.

With increasingly friendly legislators and the relaxing of acreage restrictions, the U.S. Forest Service was able to begin expanding its purchase units in Missouri.[34] In 1934, Missouri approved the expansion of initial purchase units, including the Fristoe in Carter, Oregon, Ripley, and Shannon Counties. The Forest Service also created a new purchase unit, the Wappapello in Carter, Butler, and Wayne Counties. Under the new authorizations, the Forest Service had purchase units covering 44 percent of the land in Carter and 19 percent of the land in Shannon County by the end of 1934 (fig. 23).[35] The dramatic expansion of the purchase units points to the success of people

---

[32] R. B. White to Leslie S. Bean, 9 October 1934, folder 256, Sparks Papers.

[33] R. B. White to J. N. Sparks, 9 October 1934, folder 256, Sparks Papers.

[34] Keefe, *First 50 Years*, 203.

[35] Stevens, *A Homeland and A Hinterland*, 197.

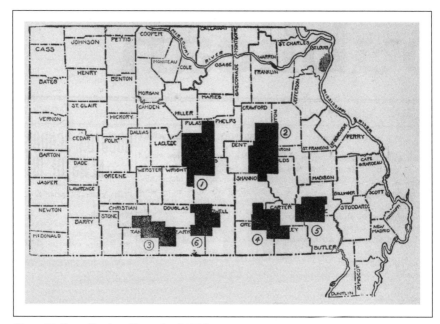

Figure 23: Forest Purchase Units, April 1934 (From *Houston Republican*, 19 April 1934, in *Missouri National Forests Association Book*, vol. 1, WHMC–Columbia).

such as Sparks and Searcy over the desires of other Ozarkers whom Bales represented.

The entrance of the Forest Service into Missouri provided dramatic benefits to the MLM. When the state legislature removed the final restrictions on the amount of land the federal government could own in individual counties, the company moved quickly. White directed Sparks, "I hope that we will be able to sell a sizable quantity of our lands for any extensions that are made to Forest units."[36] Sparks considered how the MLM could take advantage of the changes and passed his recommendations on to White, who responded, "I will execute the proposal for the 430 acres in the Wappapello Unit Extension, describing it as cutover land."[37] Few other opportunities existed for the company to dispose of unwanted land through sale. In a letter to Regional

[36] R. B. White to J. N. Sparks, 10 April 1935, folder 263, Sparks Papers.
[37] R. B. White to J. N. Sparks, 17 April 1935, folder 263, Sparks Papers.

Forester L. F. Watts, White stated, "We hereby make application for enlargement of existing Missouri units to include all of Shannon and Carter Counties." White added, "Under date of September 27th, 1935 we forwarded to Mr. Paul D. Kelleter, supervisor at St. Louis, a proposal for the sale of 49,605 acres, more or less, in Shannon County, Missouri."[38] One can only imagine what Senator Bales would have thought of White's proposal. The Forest Service and the remnants of the MLM cultivated a strong and mutually beneficial relationship as the federal government attempted to establish itself in the Courtois Hills.

Paul Delmar Kelleter, the U.S. Forest Service coordinator for Missouri and the forest supervisor for the Clark National Forest, was a key figure in the expansion of national forests in Missouri. He noted that the Forest Service had determined that roughly eight million acres in Missouri were unsuitable for agriculture and would provide the greatest good to the public as managed forests.[39] After considering the needs and opportunities in the state, the Forest Service determined, "In Missouri the present objective is the purchase of 3,363,452 acres located in 28 counties in the Ozark Region divided into eight purchase units."[40] The U.S. Forest Service acknowledged that the owners of large parcels of cutover land held the key to its ability to meet its goals.

Missouri Conservation Commission and State Forestry

When the federal government made its first entry into forest conservation in Missouri during the 1930s, the state government was close behind. Since the passage of the state's first game law in 1905, sportsmen had continued to work for the creation of an effective agency that could ensure viable game populations. Politicians, however, rejected every measure sportsmen put before the legislature. Even more galling to sportsmen than their legislative failure was the diversion of 25 percent of funds derived from the sales of hunting and

[38] R. B. White to L. F. Watts, 5 June 1935, folder 282, Sparks Papers.

[39] Paul D. Kelleter, "Formulating a New Agricultural Policy: Better Use of Our Poorer Lands as a Part of this Policy," speech notes, no date, pp. 1, 3, folder 1, Kelleter Speeches. The collection notes that it contains material exclusively from 1935 to 1940.

[40] Paul D. Kelleter, "Wildlife Research in the State and Federal Agencies: First Steps by the U.S. Forest Service," speech notes, no date, p. 1, folder 2, Kelleter Speeches. Based on context, this seems to be an early speech; in it, Kelleter states his goals without grasping the difficulties he would face in his efforts to increase the role of the federal government in Missouri.

fishing licenses after 1923 to a fund for the purchase of state parks. Hunters felt that the state should devote conservation dollars to the restocking of game animals rather than the purchase and development of parks. Sportsmen's first organized efforts to solve the problem emerged primarily among individuals affiliated with the Izaak Walton League in St. Louis. In 1935, sportsmen who had a history of conservation activities came together from across the state to create the Restoration and Conservation Federation of Missouri with the goal of establishing a state conservation commission through constitutional amendment.[41]

The federation pursued the creation of a conservation agency through a citizen-approved constitutional amendment so political leaders would not be able to defeat or subvert the new agency. The federation designed the amendment to give the commission authority to make policies for fish, wildlife, and forest conservation, and purposely left out the economic albatross of parks. Under the proposal, a four-member commission would hire all employees and have broad oversight powers. To bypass the legislature and place the amendment on the ballot for a general election the federation circulated initiative petitions for signatures in 1936. After dramatic support for the petitions emerged, the measure went on the ballot later that year as Proposition 4. In November, the proposition establishing the Missouri Conservation Commission passed with a larger majority than any proposed constitutional amendment in state history.[42]

The pattern of votes illuminates the relationship between Missourians and government. Despite Ozarkers' increasing acceptance of governmental assistance, most of the counties in the region turned the amendment down or approved it with only a slim majority. In almost the entire remainder of the state, Missourians overwhelmingly favored the proposal. This disparity reveals the continued refusal of Ozarkers to abandon their efforts to preserve some measure of autonomy in their use of the woods.

Created to conserve fish, wildlife, and forests, the Conservation Commission had to develop forest policy from scratch and add it to the established

---

[41] Callison, *Man and Wildlife*, 15–22, 24–25; Keefe, *First 50 Years*, 14–15; and Flader, *Exploring Missouri's Legacy*, 9.

[42] Callison, *Man and Wildlife*, 24, 26–27, 30–34; Keefe, *First 50 Years*, 14–21; and Flader, *Exploring Missouri's Legacy*, 9.

concerns of fish and game management. The forestry section of Missouri's official annual report for 1937–1938 stated, "Since forestry has not hitherto been a concern of the Game and Fish Department, no forestry staff is at present employed by the Commission, though it is recognized that this must be one of the first duties of the new Director."[43] Missouri looked to its past as it created a new institution.

In the spring of 1938, the Conservation Commission placed forestry in its Division of Fish, Game, and Forests and hired George O. White as the first state forester in Missouri since Dunlap had resigned in 1931.[44] White brought four years of experience with the U.S. Forest Service in Missouri to the Conservation Commission and determined to strengthen forestry in the state by cooperating with federal agencies. The commission considered White's hiring the first step towards managing the forests. In a press release in 1938, the Conservation Commission stated, "Missouri now has, for the first time in its history, facilities for a state-wide forestry program."[45] With a state forester and the fire-control and reforestation systems he would establish, Missouri once again qualified for Clarke-McNary funds. In White's first year, he acquired nearly $3,000 in federal aid for forestry. He further illustrated forestry's increasing significance by projecting that it would account for one-third of all federal funds appropriated to the Conservation Commission in Missouri for the following year.[46] As with the employment of a state forester in 1925, federal assistance seemed to provide the state with the necessary motivation to pursue conservation.

Missouri would never place large areas of land under state ownership, but after 1938 the state did possess an agency that developed the authority to create programs of forest conservation. Largely because of the lack of government-owned land in the state, Missouri faced key problems when it came to instituting conservation policies. The Forest Service identified timber theft as a

[43] "The Conservation Commission," in *State of Mo.: Official Manual . . . Nineteen Thirty-Seven and Nineteen Thirty-Eight*, 559.

[44] Press release, 2 February 1938, p. 1, Press Releases, 1937–1939, SHS Ref. Libr.; and Callison, *Man and Wildlife*, 96.

[45] Press release, 9 April 1938, p. 1, Press Releases, 1937–1939, SHS Ref. Libr.

[46] Press release, 20 March 1938; Press release, 18 April 1938, 3; and Press release, 5 May 1938, 1. All items in Press Releases, 1937–1939, SHS Ref. Libr.

preeminent challenge in the Ozarks. The agency claimed, "Shortleaf pine trees once they reach a diameter of 6 inches must be protected from timber trespass and local authorities have thus far given little assistance to the protection of land owned by nonresidents."[47] To effectively patrol and protect private lands against timber trespass, conservation agencies in Missouri increasingly found themselves forced to rely on cooperative protection agreements with private landowners.

Accordingly, one of George O. White's first actions as state forester was to create a system of four cooperative fire protection districts covering approximately two million acres in the Ozarks. He drew on his experience with the U.S. Forest Service and the past activities of Frederick Dunlap and Paul Dunn to design Missouri's system of fire prevention.[48] He built lookout towers on state lands and persuaded private landholders to join his efforts to stamp out fire. This mirrored Forest Service fire prevention and firefighting programs on the national forests in Missouri. Protection districts, made up of state, federal, and private lands, comprised the basis of White's program. Landowners agreed to fight fire and timber theft on their lands; in return, White included their properties in state plans for fire protection. The support of private landowners was necessary, because the federal and state governments owned relatively little forestland, but it left the program dependent on the holders of large tracts of land.

The U.S. Forest Service, which had cooperative firefighting agreements with the Missouri Department of Conservation, also identified woods-burning as the most significant challenge to successful forest management in the Missouri Ozarks. Fire prevention had been a central concern for forest conservation since the days of Frederick Dunlap. Forest supervisor Galen Pike tried to argue that the majority of fires during the 1930s were a byproduct of mere carelessness, but he did admit that the U.S. Forest Service had successfully convicted several Missourians under legislation directed at woods arson.[49] Richard Baumhoff, another federal forester, argued that the number of fires in Missouri grew throughout the 1930s and he opined to the St. Louis *Post-*

---

[47] *Report on Forest Conditions*, 24.

[48] Westin, "Wildfire in Missouri," 1–5. This report draws together forest fire statistics kept by the Missouri Department of Conservation from 1938 to 1991. See also Callison, *Man and Wildlife*, 96–97.

[49] Galen Pike, interview, 4–9.

Dispatch, "There are believed to be a few firebugs." He continued, "It is hard to break that habit."[50] The federal government continued its struggle to protect its forest holdings in the Ozarks. The state's Conservation Commission lacked the practical power to stamp out woods-burning during the 1930s, but it recognized the need and took the first steps to educate Ozarkers regarding the damages caused by forest fires.

Forest supervisor Kelleter commented on the behavior of local officials who turned a blind eye to woods-burning: "Such philosophy may effect re-election, but such return or continuance in office is at the very positive expense of the social and economic welfare of the communities concerned."[51] The forest supervisor recognized that Ozark politicians knew what their constituents wanted: free reign to shape the hill country as they saw fit. One of the Forest Service's first strategies to deal with woods-burning was to employ "traveling guards" who "in one or two instances have observed and caught local residents in the act of setting fire to the Government-owned land."[52] Governmental attempts to enforce the law, although frequent and in good faith, failed to end the practice of setting a torch to the woods.

State and federal forestry professionals believed the key to success in the battle against woods-burning was education. One way the Forest Service set out to convince Ozarkers to stop setting fires was to demonstrate the economic implications of such conflagrations. Kelleter pointed to studies by the Forest Service that revealed "at least 70% of the trees cut for logs and ties are defective and that 60% of such defect is readily traceable to damage by forest fires."[53] To get this message out, state and federal foresters went to "schools and public meetings of all kinds" where they presented "information of the destructive nature of fires."[54] Although foresters knew they faced an uphill battle in combating woods-burning, they thought they could educate Ozarkers to discontinue the practice.

[50] Richard G. Baumhoff, "Fighting Forest Fires," St. Louis *Post-Dispatch*, 15 April 1938.

[51] Kelleter, "Wildlife Research in the State and Federal Agencies," speech notes, no date, p. 5, folder 2, Kelleter Speeches.

[52] Kelleter, "The Clark National Forest," speech notes, no date, p. 6, folder 1, Kelleter Speeches.

[53] Kelleter, "The Clark National Forest," speech notes, no date, p. 7, folder 1, Kelleter Speeches.

[54] Kelleter, "The National Forests in Missouri," speech notes, 20 May 1935, p. 12, folder 3, Kelleter Speeches.

In addition to combating woods-burning, state and federal foresters devoted significant efforts towards reforestation programs in an attempt to shape the development of cutover lands, especially through farm forestry. Replanting began with the state nursery. In cooperation with the University of Missouri and the U.S. Forest Service, the Conservation Commission raised approximately 1,500,000 seedlings for distribution to Missouri farmers in 1938. Forestry officials specified that farmers could not plant these trees for ornamental or shade purposes but otherwise did everything possible to encourage agriculturists to participate in the program.[55] Nursery work enabled foresters to encourage the establishment of productive farm woodlots to provide protection from erosion as well as to ensure future industrial resources.

Governmental agencies utilized the practice of educating the public to the importance of forestry as a primary tool in their efforts to establish forest policies. The Conservation Commission began to publish the *Missouri Conservation News* in the late 1930s as a free service for all Missourians. In an early edition, R. S. Maddox, a forester with the Soil Conservation Service in Missouri, argued for the role of education in advancing forestry. He explained that people who knew the attributes and values of each tree species would make greater efforts to protect forests from such dangers as fire and would help save the state's soil, game, and fish.[56] By the late 1930s, Missouri's conservationists realized they could not execute forest policy without public cooperation, and they began to court public opinion. The effort to gain popular support was especially crucial for the Conservation Commission as it attempted to revitalize the timber resources of the Ozarks.

During the 1930s, state officials began to understand that the support of Ozarkers was crucial to any successful effort to establish forest policies. Demonstrating this recognition, Governor Stark informed President Franklin Roosevelt that approximately 10,000 families lived in national forest purchase units in Missouri and 400 of those families resided on land already

---

[55] Press release, 5 November 1938; Press release, 20 May 1938; and R. S. Maddox, "Forestry in Missouri," *Missouri Conservation News* (November 10, 1937): 2. All items in Press Releases, 1937–1939, SHS Ref. Libr.

[56] R. S. Maddox, "Learn to Know Trees as Good Citizens," *Missouri Conservation News* (September 1, 1937): 1, SHS Ref. Libr.

under U.S. Forest Service ownership in 1938.[57] In that year, 25 to 30 percent of all households within the Clark National Forest received support from the federal government.[58] During the Great Depression, Missourians, like people throughout the nation, relied more than ever on governmental support. This relationship between residents of the Ozarks and the federal government held the potential to facilitate forest policy in the region.

In an effort to gain more support, the Forest Service emphasized the economic benefits it planned to generate for residents of the rugged hill country. During the depths of the depression, Kelleter noted, "The plans as formulated by the Forest Service contemplate extended employment of 10,000 men in the construction of fire roads, building of telephone lines, erection of towers, elimination of fire hazards, improvement of streams, restoration of forage resources and development of areas for recreational uses." Concerned with the environmental, economic, and social health of the land and its inhabitants, the government set itself apart from the early timber industry in the Courtois Hills. Kelleter identified "impoverished communities, ghost towns, and stranded families [as] the inheritance" of corporations like the MLM.[59] Although he never named the MLM, he identified the early timber industry as responsible for much of the environmental degradation of the region. In his speeches, Kelleter demonstrated the Forest Service's growing recognition of a need to incorporate residents of the hill country in government plans for forest management and the Forest Service's wariness towards large industry.

Rural sociologist Harold Kaufman presented a good example of this evolution in federal and state policies when he argued that an "attitudinal shift" among residents of the lands to be managed was necessary if conservation was to succeed. He further theorized that this shift would only occur if conservation provided employment, range improvement, and other economic and social benefits to Ozarkers.[60] Kaufman demonstrated how conservation had changed in Missouri and what remained to be done. By the end of the

[57] Lloyd C. Stark, "Memo for the Press," 1 December 1938, p. 1, folder 6730, Stark Papers (C0004).

[58] Kaufman, "Social Factors," 3.

[59] Kelleter, "National Forests in Missouri," speech notes, 25 June 1935, pp. 2–3, folder 3, Kelleter Speeches.

[60] Kaufman, "Social Factors," 78.

1930s, governmental agencies recognized that locals needed to embrace the new policies in order for conservation to succeed in the region.

The Conservation Commission targeted the minds of the youth as fertile for conservation doctrines. Keefe explained that state and federal foresters turned to high school boys and local volunteers as the first lines of defense in firefighting and fire prevention. According to Keefe, foresters thought the most effective way to defeat the tradition of annual burning was to create a future constituency composed of locals who had personally struggled to protect the forests from fire.[61] Bill Crawford, who joined the Conservation Commission as a wildlife biologist in 1941, claimed that foresters went to local high schools for more practical reasons. He stated that schools contained the greatest number of available laborers with the physical ability to wield a rake and shovel along a fire line.[62] Robert Hargis remembered manning a fire watchtower for the Conservation Commission in 1942 when he was only fourteen years old.[63] Whether or not foresters consciously attempted to change the minds of youthful Ozarkers, the government was unable to eradicate woods-burning.

Successful implementation of forestry policies in Missouri depended in part on the state's ability to change the way previously unconvinced Ozarkers viewed the woods and hills. As part of its efforts at reforestation, Missouri struggled to make education a weapon to combat woods-burning. Keefe argued that the indoctrination of Ozarkers to the importance of fire-free woodlands went well beyond high school boys. State Forester White went directly to landowners and tried to convince them of the importance of forest management. He also undertook a campaign with a mobile film projector. The truck, projector, and generator setup became known as "The Showboat" as it toured the Ozarks presenting films to demonstrate the destructive nature of woods-burning.[64] Foresters set out to convince Ozarkers of the detrimental effects of fire and stamp out woods-burning.

[61] Keefe, *First 50 Years*, 205–7.

[62] Bill Crawford, interview.

[63] Robert Hargis and Corky Hargis, interview.

[64] Keefe, *First 50 Years*, 205–7.

Farm forestry was another area of growing concern among Missouri's foresters during the 1930s and 1940s. In 1939, the Missouri Department of Conservation began to cooperate with the Soil Conservation Service and successfully hired a farm forester. Because the Soil Conservation Service was not active in the Missouri Ozarks, this new departmental official, who was paid by both agencies, undertook his work in the northern portions of the state where projects were already under way.[65] Although this initial effort at farm forestry did not reach Ozarkers, it did demonstrate the Missouri Department of Conservation's concern with teaching private landowners how to manage their forests for the greatest profit. During the 1940s, the U.S. Forest Service assumed authority for federal farm forestry projects from the Soil Conservation Service. The Forest Service then expanded the program throughout Missouri, including the Ozarks.[66]

World War II and the Forest Cropland Law

Forestry continued to evolve in Missouri in the years leading up to and during World War II. As early as 1941, the forestry division of the Department of Conservation provided a small measure of relief to people suffering through the ramifications of an ailing economy in the rugged Ozarks by opening up jobs to facilitate the increased production of timber products associated with wartime demands.[67] During the first four years of the 1940s, timber production in the state increased by over 200 million board feet.[68] The temporary spike in production that resulted from this change in emphasis reflected the attitudes the MLM and other large timber corporations exhibited at the turn of the century. In an effort to meet shortsighted goals, the timber industry exploited the region's forests with little regard for the future.

Foresters such as Paul Kelleter who could see the long-range effects of these actions became concerned that "with the outbreak of the war and immediate demand for timber products cutting on private lands has been greatly accelerated. Many pole size stands have been clear cut leaving nothing

[65] Keefe, *First 50 Years*, 208.

[66] Ibid., 208.

[67] Ibid., 208–9.

[68] See figure 15. "The forestry work was started…," speech notes, 1944, folder 104, McCluer Papers.

to restock the area." War demands led to "devastation of the forest resources" and a more difficult situation for forest managers.[69] Other foresters argued that through effective timber management, Missouri could meet and maintain a level of productivity otherwise out of the state's grasp.[70]

During the war years of the 1940s, with their emphasis on increased timber production, some government foresters still pushed reforestation efforts. The Missouri Department of Conservation and the U.S. Forest Service had begun providing technical assistance and seedlings to cooperating private landowners as early as 1940. When war needs demanded an ever-greater portion of the Forest Service's attention, the federal government turned over control of its nursery in Missouri to the state.[71] Missouri's use of the nursery began slowly. In 1944, the state distributed just over 900,000 seedlings, almost 800,000 of which went to farmers, while Mark Twain National Forest accounted for 50,000. Carter County's sole cooperating farmer received a mere nine hundred seedlings. Farmers in several counties in northern and central Missouri obtained over fifteen thousand seedlings per county.[72] From these meager beginnings, Missouri built up an effective nursery program and expanded its cooperative programs with farmers who held the land needed future crops of timber.[73]

Despite foresters' efforts to manage and reforest timberlands, some uncooperative Ozarkers continued to exert their own form of control over the woods. In 1942 the forestry section of the Conservation Commission's annual report claimed, "In Missouri, fire is the greatest enemy to proper management of forest lands." Regardless of their repeated efforts, foresters could not defeat woods-burning.[74] Although the number of acres burned each year fluctuated, the percentage of fires attributed to arson continued to climb between 1940 and 1944. In 1944, arson surpassed debris burning as the primary recorded

[69] Kelleter, "Present Condition of Timber Stand in Missouri," speech notes, 2 July 1942, p. 2, folder, Kelleter Speeches.

[70] Schultz, "Missouri and the War," 539.

[71] Callison, *Man and Wildlife*, 100.

[72] Missouri Conservation Commission, *Annual Report... 1944*, 56–58.

[73] Press release, 17 August 1947, p. 1, and Press release, 7 September 1947, both items in Press Releases, 1946–1948, SHS Ref. Libr.

[74] Missouri Conservation Commission, *Annual Report... 1942*, 77–79.

cause of forest fires on protected lands for the first time.[75] Some Ozarkers began to accept the opportunities inherent in forest conservation by the early 1940s, but many still refused to accept government control of the woods.

Jack Toll, a lifelong Ozarker, considered the importance of burning and discussed why his neighbors eventually gave up the practice. "It stopped when the free range ended because once the free range stopped people couldn't run their livestock. The incentive to go out and burn was kinda gone because you couldn't just run your cattle out. So I imagine they went hand in hand. My guess would be that this all stopped...someplace in the early '40s."[76] In fact, Missouri would not close the open range statewide until the 1960s, but some townships and counties approved local-option laws to close the range within their borders much earlier.[77] Toll, who worked as manager of the Mingo National Wildlife Refuge in Wayne County, noted that the open range was a major issue of contention between Ozarkers and the government in the 1940s: "One of the problems they had for quite a few years with the locals was that they'd chop up the fence and let their hogs into the refuge and let them feed in there."[78] Many who resisted governmental efforts to remove land from the commons were the same folk who accepted employment or aid from the same state agencies, demonstrating the pragmatism of their forebears in the hill country.

By 1945, despite some continued resistance, Missouri's foresters were able to gain recognition for their work and began to claim roles in professional organizations. When the Ozark Section of the Society of American Foresters (including Arkansas, Oklahoma, Tennessee, Kansas, and Missouri) convened in 1945, Missouri had twenty-nine representatives from a wide variety of backgrounds. Although most of these men were employed by the Forest Service, there were also private foresters, nursery owners, and members of the Department of Conservation. Missouri's foresters gained enough respect that

---

[75] Missouri Conservation Commission, *Annual Report... 1944*, 50–55. For graphic representation of the number of fires and acres burned on an annual basis, see Westin, "Wildfire in Missouri," 26.

[76] Jack Toll, interview, 15.

[77] Rafferty, *The Ozarks*, 187.

[78] Jack Toll, interview, 15.

George O. White was elected president of the section and another forester from the state was elected chairman of the membership committee.[79]

Missouri's foresters built on their growing list of accomplishments and continued to push for a comprehensive program of management for the state's forests after the war was over. The timber industry and foresters worked together to retain the increased importance they had achieved during the war years. In 1946, the forestry section of Missouri's annual report argued that the objective of state forestry was still "maintaining lumber production at a high level."[80] Foresters' awareness of the conservation of forests and the welfare of those who lived on the land to be managed may have increased during the 1930s and 1940s, but industrial production was still the agenda. This seems largely traceable to the state's recognition that it needed industrial support to successfully institute forest policy.

After about a decade of activity, the state's forestry division gained a significant victory in 1946. Missouri's foresters had labored with many difficult situations; one of the most significant was that private landowners held approximately 90 percent of forestland in the state.[81] The General Assembly finally responded to the entreaties of conservationists by enacting a bill that became known as the Forest Cropland Law. Albert Kraemalmeyer of Crawford County (located on the northeastern edge of the Missouri Ozarks), the bill's author, set out to remedy the inequities of real estate taxation so private landholders could manage their forests for future gains.[82] Representative C. P. Turley of Carter County and Kraemalmeyer emerged as the bill's champions and ushered it through the House with no debate.[83] After emerging from the House, the bill went to the Senate where it won with a vote of twenty-seven to zero.[84]

[79] Newsletter: The Society of American Foresters, Ozark Section, 14 May 1945, folder 196, Dunlap Papers.

[80] "Missouri Forests," in *State of Mo.: Official Manual… Nineteen Forty-Five and Nineteen Forty-Six*, 665.

[81] Keefe, *First 50 Years*, 206.

[82] Callison, *Man and Wildlife*, 100; "Report of the Forestry Division," in *State of Mo.: Official Manual… Nineteen Forty-Seven and Nineteen Forty-Eight*, 281–82.

[83] "House Advances Bill to Restore State's Forests," St. Louis *Post-Dispatch*, 6 June 1946; And Lew Larkin, "A Forestry Bill Ahead," Kansas City *Times*, 12 June 1946.

[84] "Forest Conservation Wins 27–0 in Senate Vote," *Daily Capital News*, 26 June 1946.

The mechanics of this bill help explain why it gained such strong support. The Forest Cropland Law advanced the cause of forestry in Missouri by addressing the tax problems Governor Folk and the Missouri Forestry Commission had identified in the first decade of the century. Landowners who participated in the program received complete exemption from state taxes on their forestland for twenty-five years or an assessment value of one dollar per acre, depending on the value of the woodlands and the size of the tract. Landowners who harvested their timber during that period paid a yield tax based on the increased value of the timber. State forester White believed that the relaxation of taxes would be the deciding factor in encouraging private landholders to manage their forests for the future.[85] To offset the decreased local tax base, the state provided counties with two cents per acre entered in the program. To meet this financial responsibility, the state appropriated $100,000 to start a revolving fund that would be replenished by yield tax payments from timber harvested from lands designated as forest cropland.[86] This program gave the state a vehicle through which it could improve the quality of standing forests, encourage reforestation, and do it (in characteristic Missouri fashion) by spending very little money.

The Missouri legislature passed the Forest Cropland Law in June 1946, but a constitutional technicality prevented the governor from approving the necessary appropriations. One year later, June 1947, with the measure now approved, the first agreements became official. The initial participation brought approximately 135,000 acres into the program and called for the transfer of almost $5,000 to county governments at the amended rate of reimbursement, four cents per acre. Shannon County received the largest payment at approximately $1,601 for its 40,027 acres in the program.[87] This promise of state money for county coffers likely explains Representative Turley's strong support.

[85] "Signs a Forestry Bill," Kansas City *Times*, 6 July 1946; and Keefe, *First 50 Years*, 206.

[86] "State Forestry Bill Passed by Missouri Assembly," St. Louis *Star Tribune*, 27 June 1946; "Governor Signs First Statewide Forestry Bill," *Daily Capital News*, 6 July 1946; and "For a State of Great Forests," Kansas City *Star*, 8 July 1946.

[87] Keefe, *First 50 Years*, 206; "To Implement the Forestry Act," St. Louis *Globe-Democrat*, 31 August 1946; "For a State of Great Forests," Kansas City *Star*, 3 September 1946; and Robert E. Holliway, "Commission Okays Tracts for State Forestry Benefits," St. Louis *Star*, 6 June 1947.

Missouri's foresters and conservationists continued to push for a more comprehensive management strategy after the Forest Cropland Law was in place. In 1946, the Kansas City *Star* covered a forestry conference in Jefferson City where Shirley W. Allen, president of the Society of American Foresters, reported that Missouri's forests could add $500 million to the state's economy if they were managed correctly.[88] The *Daily Capital News* also covered the conference and noted that Allen argued, "Only one-tenth of Missouri's great forest potential is under good management at present."[89] As the head of the leading professional organization for foresters, Allen certainly held the attention of Missouri's foresters. Because there were fewer than forty thousand acres of state-owned forests in Missouri, foresters seeking to develop the economic potential of timberlands statewide had to direct their management strategies towards cooperation with private landowners.[90]

With a forestry law in place and a developing spirit of cooperation between landowners, the U.S. Forest Service, and the Missouri Department of Conservation, it seemed as if forestry had a solid foundation in Missouri. The state's conservation agency was written into the constitution and forestry was a major part of it, but it was still far from well entrenched by the end of the 1940s. Many challenges remained in the rugged portions of the Ozarks.

[88] "Missouri Is Tree Rich," Kansas City *Star*, 14 November 1946.

[89] "Forest Problem: Understanding Is State Need," *Daily Capital News*, 15 November 1946.

[90] Keefe, *First 50 Years*, 208–9.

Chapter 6

A Twentieth-Century Epilogue

Missouri moved into the 1950s with a well-established forestry agency and the legislative machinery to expand its influence in the Ozarks. Many Missourians were not ready, however, to turn control of their woodlands over to the state. During the second half of the twentieth century, Ozarkers increasingly accepted elements of governmental conservation despite continued struggles over who would control the utilization of the region's forests.

Conflicts Over Conservation and Forest Control

A series of challenges to the Missouri Conservation Commission in the late 1940s and early 1950s indicated that conservation was not completely established in the state. The St. Louis *Globe-Democrat* reported in 1949, "Another move to strip the Missouri Conservation Commission of its powers was begun in the General Assembly today."[1] The Jefferson City *Post-Tribune* noted that this was the sixth failed attempt in the past twelve years to reduce the power of the Conservation Commission. The commission was able to fight off these attacks and retain its power, largely because, as the *Post-Tribune* stated, "When five members of the Missouri House of Representatives introduced a

---

[1] "Bill Offered to Strip the Conservation Board of Regulatory Power," St. Louis *Globe-Democrat*, 10 February 1949.

bill to sabotage the State Conservation Commission they invited the wrath of the state's conservationists and sportsmen."[2] The Conservation Commission staved off these early challenges, but was unable to truly solidify its position in state government.

In March 1953, two representatives introduced another measure to remove the commission's power to establish conservation policies and select employees, proposing to return these powers to the General Assembly. The two men, representatives from the Ozark counties of Crawford and Dallas, attempted to halt the Conservation Commission from gaining the power to control access to the region's forests. A key component of the proposed amendment was that the legislature would have the power to set the cost of hunting and fishing licenses and the proceeds would go to the counties rather than to the conservation agency. This aspect of the bill appealed to poor Missourians, of which there were many in the Courtois Hills, who hoped for lower license fees.[3] When the measure made it out of the committee, the full house barely defeated it with a vote of fifty-three to fifty-two.[4]

After this narrow vote, the issue of who would control conservation was not settled. In April, a constitutional amendment to place all powers of employment, policy, and enforcement regarding conservation in the hands of the General Assembly came before the Forestry, Fish, and Game Committee. The committee voted down this latest of the house's four attempted power grabs during the session.[5] When Missouri's voters created the Conservation Commission, politicians lost any power they had enjoyed over the selection of individuals to what were previously patronage positions. Sportsmen and other supporters argued that the Conservation Commission freed them from constant battles with the General Assembly to keep the department free from politics.[6] In its early years, the Conservation Commission had not only had to deal with recalcitrant residents of the Ozarks and ambitious timbermen,

[2] "Missouri Sportsmen Speak Out," Jefferson City *Post-Tribune*, 22 February 1949.

[3] "New Grab at Conservation Agency Gets Started in Missouri House," St. Louis *Post-Dispatch*, 6 March 1953.

[4] "Hunting License Bill Killed," *Daily Capital News*, 11 March 1953.

[5] "Move to Give Conservation Power to Legislature Defeated Again," St. Louis *Post-Dispatch*, 24 April 1953.

[6] Bill Crawford, interview.

but also with legislators who resented their loss of control over game and fish policies.

Foresters continued to adhere to the belief that they had the knowledge and the ability to help Missourians if the state's citizens would only cooperate. State Forester George O. White reported that forty-seven private landholders were cooperating with the state through the Forest Cropland Law by summer 1953. This cooperation brought 204,977 acres under some form of management.[7] The next year, Franklin G. Liming, employed by the U.S. Forest Service at its research station in Columbia, Missouri, declared that the state was only producing one-fifth to one-third of the timber it could produce under good management.[8] Foresters were determined to expand their influence throughout Missouri's forestlands.

Fire remained the most significant issue for forest control in the Missouri Ozarks. Despite the Department of Conservation's efforts, the state had yet to gain complete control of its timberlands by the end of the century. Missourians

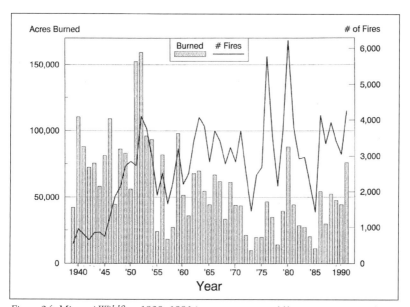

Figure 24: Missouri Wildfires 1939–1991 (From Westin, "Wildfire in Missouri," 26).

[7] "Forest Crop Area Up," Kansas City *Times*, 18 August 1953.
[8] "Urges Better Use of Ozark Forests," St. Louis *Post-Dispatch*, 12 April 1954.

continued to burn the woods to meet their needs, desires, or simply out of spite. The incidence of fire, however, has decreased over the years (fig. 24).

One key to consider in interpreting the Department of Conservation's statistics on forest fires is the amount of land the figures include. One problem for comparing statistics is that the number of acres protected by the Missouri Department of Conservation continued to increase. Early statistics counted fires only on the acreage of land included in fire protection districts, which did not surpass five million acres until the late 1940s. These districts were composed of state lands and private forests that were entered into cooperative firefighting agreements. Then in the mid-1970s, the Department of Conservation began keeping statistics for fires throughout the timberlands of the entire state, which amounted to approximately 16 million acres. Finally, in the early 1990s the statistics began to include all of Missouri's 44 million acres.[9]

The number of fires fluctuated widely from year to year. Weather remained a key factor in the severity of wildfires in Missouri. In 1952, the Department of Conservation recorded the highest number of fires and acres burned on protected lands to date, even though the department only had cooperative firefighting agreements covering a small portion of the state.[10] Three years later, in 1955, the acreage lost to fire dropped radically to one of the lowest years in history. It is unclear why 1955 witnessed such a small burn. One possible explanation is that the previous four years had been some of the state's most severe fire years on record, and were also a period of serious drought. When the drought ended, the return of rain and green foliage in 1955, combined with debris loads that had been diminished by preceding heavy burns, meant that there was little debris to burn and the moisture was not conducive to significant spreading of fires.[11]

A line of best fit plotted for the graph in figure 24 demonstrates a moderate downward slope that becomes more significant when compared with the rising slope of the line depicting the number of acres protected. Therefore, even though the acreage burned does not decrease dramatically, the percentage of protected land burned annually does drop noticeably. The Department

[9] Westin, "Wildfire in Missouri," 1–3, 24–25.

[10] Ibid., 24–26.

[11] Ibid., 26; "1954 Drought Hard on Missouri Trees," St. Louis *Post-Dispatch*, 27 December 1954; and "Few Fires in Forest," Kansas City *Star*, 9 September 1955.

of Conservation continued to face bad fire years such as those in 1951 to 1954, especially in 1959, 1980, and 1991, but the years of devastation became increasingly less frequent and less severe.[12]

The cause of fires continued to present foresters in Missouri with a much more significant problem than the mere high number of acres burned. The St. Louis *Post-Dispatch* reported in 1954, "Of the 4615 fires on protected lands, 2196 were attributed to careless debris burners and 1305 were described as having been set by incendiarists."[13] Despite nearly two decades of concerted efforts by the Forest Service and the Conservation Commission, fire remained a significant problem. Debris-burning is an intriguing category. The possibility exists that many of the fires so classified were in reality arson. What some people may have identified as debris-burning could have been called woods-burning by others.

Human-set fires continued as a controversial element in the woods of the Courtois Hills and throughout the Ozarks. In 1956, the Jefferson City *Post-Tribune* reported, "Most Missouri fires are caused by burning trash without taking proper precautions, and a number have been started by hunters trying to smoke game out with bonfires." The newspaper based its assessment on an interview with Osal Capps, chief of the fire control section of the Conservation Commission.[14] The frequency of fire due to carelessness demonstrates the degree to which many Missourians ignored, if not outright rejected, the continuing efforts of the Conservation Commission to stress management and protection of the state's forests. The 1950s, however, was a decade in which the Department of Conservation witnessed a general improvement in its success in fighting fires.

In the 1960s, fire continued to play an important role in forest policy, but a new issue—the open range—came to the fore. In 1965, two key developments occurred in the drive to end woodland grazing in the Ozarks. One development was the Forest Service's announcement in February 1965 that it would close the open range on its lands as of 31 October. Wayne Leeman of the St. Louis

[12] Westin, "Wildfire in Missouri," 1–26.

[13] "957,379 Acres Of Missouri Forests Burned Last Year," St. Louis *Post-Dispatch*, 8 July 1954.

[14] "Forest Fire Loss Up Sharply In Missouri," St. Louis *Post-Dispatch*, 16 January1953; "1956 Bad Year for Forest Fire Damage in State," Jefferson City *Post-Tribune*, 14 September 1956; and Westin, "Wildfire in Missouri," 12, 26.

Post-Dispatch detailed the other development based on information he gathered when he interviewed Leon Hornkohl, the Forest Service's land management specialist in Rolla, Missouri. Leeman reported, "In the last general election, five townships in Carter County were closed to complete coverage in that county and a favorable vote for closed range was recorded in Wayne, Shannon, Washington, Dent and Iron." Hornkohl also told Leeman that despite the townships that voted for closure, the largest tracts of open range remaining in the state were in Shannon and Ripley Counties, and that Shannon County had voted down a countywide measure to close the range the previous November.[15] Shannon and Ripley Counties, well within the Courtois Hills, were the last counties in Missouri to sustain open-range grazing.

One of the most significant aspects of Leeman's article is the connection Leon Hornkohl drew between the open range and forest fires. Hornkohl discussed a group of citizens who attempted to get the closed range reopened in Washington County, but failed. Leeman quoted Hornkohl, "The significance to me is that good citizens now can vote for closed range without fear of retaliation." This is an enlightening indication of the social climate in the county. Reform elements had gained enough control in the region to close the range without fear of retribution from residents who felt a strong connection to their generations-old practices. Hornkohl also stated, "Possibly of equal importance is the fact that these same citizens now are showing a willingness to testify in forest fire cases. For many years there has been much reticence in this area."[16] Once they closed the range, reformers in Washington County also successfully and safely began to attack the closely allied institution of woods-burning. The open range and woods-burning combined to characterize local subsistence-level relationships with the hill country. With the loss of the open range, the incentive to use fire to improve the forest grasses, on which unfenced cattle had depended, no longer remained.

That same year, a bill to close the range statewide came before the House Agricultural Committee. The committee heard the arguments of several people from Carter County who opposed the measure. After listening to the testimony,

---

[15] Wayne Leeman, "End of Open Range in Missouri Expected Within a Few Years," St. Louis *Post-Dispatch*, 23 February 1965.

[16] Ibid.

the committee voted nineteen to seventeen to keep the range open. The St. Louis *Post-Dispatch* summed up the concerns of the individuals from Carter County: "Without open range, many Ozark farmers will be forced to sell their cattle and hogs." The paper also noted that the Carter County residents claimed, "This will reduce the personal property tax rolls and deprive many persons of a livelihood." The residents of the hill country who could not afford to buy sufficient grazing land or soil for intensive agriculture now faced a crisis spawned of a legislated change in subsistence practices. Reformers in the state government saw the issue from a different perspective. According to the *Post-Dispatch*, Representative Charles B. James of Dunklin County, who sponsored the bill to close the range, spoke of Ozarkers: "The Legislature would do these persons a favor by abolishing the open range."[17] His remarks repeated the attitude and argument of Thomas T. Hathaway of St. Louis, who as early as 1873 had called for a statewide closure of the range.

A bill to close the range statewide finally passed the legislature and was signed into law in 1969.[18] Protracted controversy over the open range reflects the conflicts inherent in many conservation issues. Reformers, whether they were affiliated with the timber industry, a forestry association, or a legislative body, believed they had the ability and knowledge to tell residents of the Courtois Hills and other areas how to interact with the woods. Many of these rural Missourians, however, believed the traditions that had worked for their ancestors would continue to provide sustenance and satisfaction into the future. By no means, however, has life in the Ozarks been an unchanging proposition. Residents of the region chose which elements of their lives to change in the face of conflict, continuing to demonstrate a pragmatic relationship with the representatives of opposing belief systems.

There was a new element by the 1960s that lent a new weight to the fight to close the range. One of the strongest supporters of a closed range was Colonel Hugh Waggoner, the head of the Missouri State Highway Patrol. Waggoner had his troopers note whether automobile/livestock accidents occurred in closed or open range townships to attribute responsibility. In townships where fence laws were in effect, the stock owner was liable to the driver,

---

[17] "Open Range Losing Ground Despite Vote," St. Louis *Post-Dispatch*, 31 March 1965.

[18] Stevens, *A Homeland and A Hinterland*, 204–5.

whereas in townships with open range, it was the driver who had financial responsibility to the stock owner.[19] During the 1920s, the federal and state governments began to put money into improving roadways in the rugged portions of the Missouri Ozarks, tourism increased, and local ownership of automobiles became more widespread. By the end of World War II, roadways were further improved to allow for high-speed travel.[20] Once a greater number of drivers began to travel rapidly through the hilly, open-range country, automobile/livestock accidents became a greater concern. This may have been one of the precipitating factors behind statewide closure of the range in 1969.

One area of persistent conflict began to take on a new appearance in the late 1960s, as professional foresters in Missouri began to study the ecological role of fire and to discuss its practical uses. Fire had long been an issue of contention among foresters throughout the nation. In a study of attitudes towards fire within the U.S. Forest Service, Ashley Schiff relayed the agency's position at the beginning of the twentieth century: "Prevent fire, exclude hogs, leave ample seed trees, and nature herself would restore longleaf to its primeval state."[21] Foresters in Missouri shared this desire to eliminate fire in the state's shortleaf pine forests where hogs and cattle roamed freely and fires ran wild each year. During the 1920s, dissension over fire had become increasingly heated as some foresters began to argue for the importance of controlled burns in the maintenance of certain forest types, particularly longleaf pine. Until well into the 1930s, however, the Forest Service made the elimination of fires in all forests one of its main goals. As the Forest Service and other forestry associations began to conduct more research on the role of fire, prescribed burning slowly moved into the forester's toolbox. In 1943, elements within the Forest Service acknowledged the potential benefits of controlled burns and, in some cases, allowed foresters to use fire within national forests.[22]

Missourians witnessed the growing national debate on the role of controlled fire in the forests and slowly began to experiment with the technique.

---

[19] Leeman, "End of Open Range in Missouri," St. Louis *Post-Dispatch*, 23 February 1965.

[20] Stevens, *A Homeland and A Hinterland*, 167–96.

[21] Schiff, *Fire and Water*, 16.

[22] Schiff, *Fire and Water*, 36–37, 43–44, 83, 98; and Pyne, *Fire in America*.

Some of the early practical studies of the role of fire in the Ozarks began with the establishment of experiment and control plots in 1949 and 1951 on the University of Missouri's University Forest in Butler County. Foresters utilized these plots to undertake a long-term study of the effects of annual and periodic (once every five years) fires on hardwood stands.[23] In 1966, Paul Scowcroft compiled an assessment of the Department of Conservation's experiments with these controlled burns. Two of his conclusions supported annual burning as practiced historically. Scowcroft found that both periodic and annual burning decreased forest litter and significantly increased the growth of grasses. Although these two points supported burning as a means of preparing the forest for open-range grazing, Scowcroft was opposed to woods-burning. He concluded that both types of fire led to slower tree growth, extensive scarring, and high mortality, especially among the more marketable species of Ozark hardwoods. In addition to these negative results, he argued that fire also removed protective vegetation from the soil allowing for compaction through the mechanical process of raindrop impaction.[24] In this early study, regular fire appeared as an unwanted agent in timberlands.

In 1974, Calvin Meier followed Scowcroft with an analysis of fire in the Ozarks based largely on the same body of evidence. Meier studied the region from the perspective of the relationship between timber cover and soils, and concluded, "The severe annual burn does not appear to be a satisfactory management tool." In essence, he agreed with Scowcroft. Unlike Scowcroft, however, he felt that the periodic burn "may be useful in some instances." Although this was far from a ringing endorsement for the use of fire, Meier acknowledged controlled burning as a potential tool. In his concluding paragraph, Meier argued against the use of annual fire but claimed that periodic fire offered more positives than negatives when used properly.[25]

Despite an accumulating body of literature on the subject, the Department of Conservation was hesitant to employ controlled burning, especially in

---

[23] Scowcroft, "Effects of Fire," 2–3. George Hartman, fire ecologist for the Missouri Department of Conservation, considers the University Forest burning experiments of national significance primarily because of their duration. The Department of Conservation has continued the procedures for over five decades and created a formidable body of data concerning the role of fire in hardwood forests; Hartman, interview.

[24] Scowcroft, "Effects of Fire," 18, 23, 121–22.

[25] Meier, "Effect of Fire," 74, 77.

view of its decades-long efforts to stamp out woods-burning. The department's forestry division would not hire its first fire ecologist until 1994. Even then, foresters continued to encounter problems. Many rural Missourians resented the fact that the same agency that spent decades prosecuting them for setting fires was now burning the forests.[26]

Well into the twentieth century, Missouri's forests continued to face many challenges, but the state's foresters pointed to definite improvement. In 1972, the department estimated that sawtimber (eleven inches in diameter at breast height in hardwood or nine inches in softwood) and pole-timber each accounted for 39 percent of Missouri's timberlands. Sapling or seedling stands made up the remaining 22 percent. By 1989, the sawtimber component of timberlands in the state increased to approximately 49 percent, while pole-timber decreased to 29 percent and sapling and seedling stands remained essentially constant.[27] Thomas L. Schmidt, a research forester for the U.S. Forest Service's North Central Research Station in St. Paul, prepared a report in 1999 in which he assessed Missouri's forests. He noted that the state's forests contained approximately 1.2 billion cubic feet of wood in conifers and 12.5 billion cubic feet of hardwoods in 1999 compared to only 300,000 cubic feet in conifers and a mere 4 billion in hardwoods in 1947. He also demonstrated that this increase occurred at a continuous rate with no significant period of forest retreat.[28] This optimism marks much of the literature the Department of Conservation and the U.S. Forest Service produced in relation to Missouri's forests in the second half of the twentieth century. Foresters maintained their faith in the future of managed, sustainable production.

But other data point to a need for significantly more and better oversight. Due to generations of woods-burning, open-range grazing, and overcutting, Missouri's forests at the end of the century were composed of a high percentage of trees that are rough, rotten, or genetically inferior and therefore unsuitable for timber production. Some foresters argue that the poor quality of these trees and the increasing age of timber stands throughout Missouri's

---

[26] George Hartman, interview; and Lynn Barnickol, interview. Hartman is fire ecologist for the Missouri Department of Conservation and Barnickol is a forest supervisor and forest products specialist for the Missouri Department of Conservation.

[27] Spencer, Roussopoulos, and Massengale, *Missouri's Forest Resource, 1989*, 6.

[28] Schmidt, "Missouri's Forest Resources in 1999," 3–5.

forests are some of the most important factors in the state's problem of oak decline.[29]

Arson remains a more persistent problem. The clearest measure of the Department of Conservation's success in fire suppression is the decrease in the average size of wildfires (fig. 25). Foresters have shortened their response time, but even more importantly, residents of the hill country have begun to report fires. Despite notable achievements in reducing wildland fire, an analysis of the fires in Missouri in 2000 provides some insight into the problems the Department of Conservation faced at the end of the century. In that year, the top five causes of wildland fire were debris burning (2,624 fires on 46,604 acres), miscellaneous (921 fires on 17,759 acres), arson (832 fires on 61,197 acres), ignitions from the heat or sparks of gasoline-powered equipment (216 fires on 2,166 acres), and campfires that escaped control (34 fires on 1,086 acres). Averaging approximately 73.5 acres per fire, arson fires accounted for by far the largest area per burn. One possible explanation for this is that

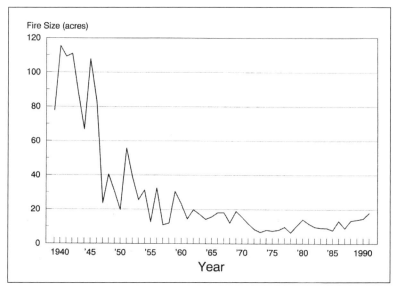

Figure 25: Average Wildfire Size in Missouri, 1939–1991 (From Westin, "Wildfire in Missouri," 28).

[29] Lynn Barnickol, interview. For a brief discussion of oak decline, see Lawrence, Moltzan, and Moser, "Oak Decline."

arsonists intentionally set fires for the greatest effect and their neighbors may have helped, or at least not reported the fires because they agreed with the fire-starters. One Department of Conservation estimate placed arson as the cause of 50 percent of the fires in Missouri's woodlands.[30]

An Ever-Evolving Region Continues On

Missouri's timber industry moved from boom to bust to gradual reestablishment, largely within the Courtois Hills region of the Ozarks. The residents of this region, whether locals by way of generations of persistence or newcomers, picked and chose from the opportunities offered by self-subsistence and industrial employment. Residents turned to the Missouri Lumber and Mining Company and its contemporaries for paychecks and goods they could not easily make or obtain from their fellow hill folk. Strategies of self-subsistence and independence retained enough appeal even for many newcomers that the "civilization" proposed by industrialists only emerged in the region on a piecemeal basis.

After the timber companies had exploited the valuable shortleaf pine of the Courtois Hills, they disposed of the cutover land as quickly as possible and moved on. Those residents who remained behind attempted to resurrect a lifestyle of small-scale farming supplemented by open-range grazing and hunting. Unfortunately for these struggling farmers, the cutover hills could no longer support their heavy reliance on the woods.

The state and federal governments attempted to establish resource policies for the impoverished portions of the Ozarks, but faced significant resistance. The still-powerful timber industry gained control of the state's early efforts at conservation and stymied federal involvement in Missouri's forests during the 1920s. This situation did not change until the precipitous decline of the industry coincided with an increasing sentiment among Missourians statewide for conservation and with the growing willingness of professional resource managers to address the needs of economically desperate rural people. A number of successful programs affiliated with such agencies as the Civilian Conservation Corps, the U.S. Forest Service, and the Missouri Department of Conservation offered opportunities for residents of the Courtois Hills

[30] Mo. Department of Conservation, State Fire Marshall, *Living With Wildfire*, 7.

and other rural areas to become increasingly amenable towards governmental intervention in the woods.

Government agents recognized the environmental and economic crises of rural Missouri, in many cases reflected in sharp detail in the rugged Ozarks. Those who chose to call the Courtois Hills home treated the woods as a communal resource for hunting, gathering, and the grazing of livestock. A crucial and controversial component of this attitude was the need to burn the hills each spring to maintain the woods in a desirable condition. Both the federal and state governments attempted valiantly to end the trinity of ills: woods-burning, timber theft, and poaching. Despite their attachment to traditional ways, residents of the region were far from resistant to the modern world. They chose to accept those elements of the market economy and of resource management they could fit into their worldviews, yet simultaneously fought to preserve their image of the hill country and their place within it.

Even at the end of the twentieth century, no one could claim complete control of Missouri's Ozark forests. The state still maintained a viable timber industry, however diminished and fragmented, but no companies dominated the scene. The state and federal government have each obtained more land for forests and parks, although their combined holdings equal no more than 15 percent of the timberlands in Missouri. Residents of the hill country remained closely tied to their woods and their desire for independence and still filtered social and environmental opportunities through the lens of locale.

An analysis of the history of the Missouri Ozarks, and the Courtois Hills in particular, foreshadows many current issues facing policy-makers who deal with resource-dependent communities. Such communities pose a wide range of management problems, whether the impact of global climate change and oil spills on salmon fisheries, restrictions on pesticide and herbicide use on federal-lease lands for agriculture, or the diminution of—and listing of endangered species in—old-growth forests. Natural-resource managers are confronted with creating and maintaining a balance between exploitation and conservation to perpetuate stability in the community and the resource.

In the early 1990s, the U.S. Forest Service attempted to assist timber-dependent communities in the Pacific Northwest that were facing decreasing timber sales by changing the focus of its management strategies. The Forest Service began to plan its management strategies with the economic stability of dependent communities as a primary, rather than a secondary, concern. Since the 1990s, the Forest Service has continued to refine its mission and build closer relationships with timber-dependent communities throughout the nation.

Change inevitably comes to most resource-dependent communities. In a guide to communities going through the loss of their resource base, sociologist Flaxen D. L. Conway recommended, "We must go with the flow rather than fight against it. Going with the flow doesn't mean giving up. The key is to keep a firm grasp on our core beliefs and values while we adapt to the changing scenery and circumstances of our lives. New skills and tools can help us manage these changes."[31] The residents of the Courtois Hills went "with the flow" during the heyday of the Missouri Lumber and Mining Company, while trying desperately to hold to their core beliefs and values. Unfortunately for the residents and the forests, timber companies cut the timber with no thoughts of long-term profits, leaving locals with a drastically depleted environment.

A successful solution to the problems of resource-dependent communities, as demonstrated in Carter County, cannot be found in the actions of government alone. Industry must accept sustainable use, whether fish, soil, timber, or any other resource. Even the most well-planned and well-intentioned policies, however, will not succeed without the support of the residents of the region to be managed. In the Courtois Hills, local residents accepted jobs in the industry, but only accepted the social changes they found to complement existing beliefs. Neither would they allow government to reduce their access to the woods without recognizing their economic needs.

The Missouri Ozarks underwent another dramatic change at the end of the twentieth century. After nearly a century of population decline, rural Missouri began to gain residents. This new trend was coupled with slow growth statewide. In the 1990s, the state's population increased by approximately 9 percent, with rural areas exceeding that rate by almost two percentage points. This rural growth was more pronounced in the Ozarks, because the state's other two major rural areas, the Bootheel and northern Missouri, have experienced more severe economic challenges and some counties there

---

[31] Conway, Corcoran, and Tillson, *Towns in Transition*, 9. Conway draws on Theobald, *The Rapids of Change*.

have remained static or declined. By choosing to settle disproportionately in the woods and on the hillsides of the Ozarks, the new immigrants have contributed to a pattern where over 70 percent of the growth in Missouri's rural counties occurred outside the boundaries of incorporated towns and cities. As with other times of change in the region, the definition of Ozarker has expanded and the possibility of a new relationship with the woods has emerged.[32]

---

[32] Center on Urban and Metropolitan Policy, *Growth in the Heartland.*

Works Cited

Archives

CCC Camp No. 3737 Papers   Civilian Conservation Corps (U.S.), Camp No. 3737 (Lynchburg, MO) WHMC Collection, 1935–1983. (R177), WHMC–Rolla

Dunlap Papers   Frederick Dunlap (1881–1968) Papers, 1891–1937 (C2606), WHMC–Columbia

Hadley Papers   Herbert Spencer Hadley (1830–1943) Papers, 1872–1927 (C0006), WHMC–Columbia

Kelleter Speeches   Paul Delmar Kelleter (1891–1950) Speeches, 1935–1940 (C2249), WHMC–Columbia

McCluer Papers   Franc L. McCluer (1896–1979) Constitutional Convention Papers, 1943-1944 (C0022), WHMC–Columbia

MLM Records   Missouri Lumber and Mining Company Records, 1853–1945 (C2557), WHMC–Columbia

MLM Photographs   Missouri Lumber and Mining Company, Photographs, 1906–1916 (C3875), WHMC–Columbia

SHS Ref. Libr.   State Historical Society of Missouri, Reference Library, Columbia, MO

Sparks Papers   John Nathan Sparks (1876–?) Papers, 1901–1947 (C2798), WHMC–Columbia

Stark Papers (C0004)   Lloyd Crow Stark (1886–1972) Papers, 1931–1941 (C0004), WHMC–Columbia

WHMC   Western History Manuscripts Collection

WHMC–Columbia, Ellis Library, University of Missouri–Columbia

WHMC–Rolla, Curtis Laws Wilson Library, Missouri University of Science and Technology

Interviews

Barnickol, Lynn. Interview by David Benac, 6 February 2003.

Baugh, Roy. Interview by Alexander Primm, 23 April 1992.

Blackwell, Wayne, and Icelene Blackwell. Interviewed by C. C. Modi and Sadi Negaard, 5 January 1978. 1-1-243, Box 16, Folder 14, Center for Ozark Studies Collection, Record Group 8.11, Department of Special Collections and Archives, Duane G. Meyer Library, Southwest Missouri University, Springfield, MO.

Crawford, Bill. Interview by David Benac, 21 January 2003.

Dablemont, Ferrel. Interview by Alexander Primm, 12 May 1998.

Dettwiler, Ab. Interview by Alexander Primm, 23 April 1992.

Dunn, Paul M. "St. Regis Paper Company: An Oral History Interview." Interview by Elwood R. Maunder. Santa Cruz, CA: Forest History Society, 1977.

Hargis, Robert, and "Corky" Hargis. Interview by Alexander Primm, 6 November 1997.

Hartman, George. Interview by David Benac, 7 April 2003.

Horgan, Lon. Interviewer unidentified, 29 August 1979. Center for Ozark Studies Collection, Record Group 8.11, Department of Special Collections and Archives, Duane G. Meyer Library, Southwest Missouri University, Springfield, MO.

Martin, Tom, and Minnie Martin. Interview by Alexander Primm, 19–20 May 1992.

Pike, Galen. Interviewer unidentified, 31 August 1936. Interview part of a series conducted by KWTO radio station in Springfield, MO. Transcript in folder 4, Mark Twain National Forest (MO), Local History Collection (R471), WHMC–Rolla.

Toll, Jack. Interview by Alexander Primm, 27 May 1992.

[Note: Interviews by Primm in private collection of interviewer; transcriptions of Primm interviews by David Benac, in possession of author.]

Published Works

"An Act Creating a Forestry Board and Making an Appropriation Therefor." In *Appendix to the House and Senate Journals...1909*, sect. 38, pp. 13–15.

Appendix to the House and State Senate Journals of the 45th General Assembly of the State of Missouri, 1909. Jefferson City, MO: Hugh Stephens Printing Co., 1909.

Arnesen, Eric. *Brotherhoods of Color: Black Railroad Workers and the Struggle for Equality.* Cambridge, MA: Harvard University Press, 2001.

Baldwin, Sara Mullin. *Who's Who in Kansas City, 1930: Biographical sketches of men and women of achievement.* Hebron, NE: Baldwin, 1930.

Blair, Karen J. *The Clubwoman as Feminist: True Womanhood Redefined, 1868–1914.* New York: Holmes & Meier Publishers, 1980.

Blanchard, Newton C., et al., eds. *Proceedings of a Conference of Governors in the White House, Washington, D.C., May 13–15, 1908.* Washington, DC: Government Printing Office, 1909.

Blevins, Brooks. *Hill Folks: A History of Arkansas Ozarkers and Their Image.* Chapel Hill: University of North Carolina Press, 2001.

Buford, Wilbur C. *Annual Report of the State Game and Fish Commissioner to the Honorable*

Guy B. Park, Governor of the State of Missouri, For the Year Ending December 31, 1933. Jefferson City: Midland Printing Co., 1934.

———. *Annual Report of the State Game and Fish Commissioner to the Honorable Lloyd C. Stark, Governor of the State of Missouri, For the Year Ending December 31, 1935.* Jefferson City: Midland Printing Co., 1936.

Callison, Charles H. *Man and Wildlife: The History of One State's Treatment of Its Natural Resources.* Harrisburg, PA: Stackpole, 1953.

Center on Urban and Metropolitan Policy. *Growth in the Heartland: Challenges and Opportunities for Missouri.* Washington, DC: Brookings Institution, December 2002.

Chandler, Alfred D. *The Visible Hand: The Managerial Revolution in American Business.* Cambridge, MA: Belknap Press, 1977.

Chapman, C. S. "Methods Which Should Be Adopted by Private Owners." In *Report of the National Conservation Commission, February 1909*, vol. 2, edited by Henry Gannett, 711–24. Washington, DC: Government Printing Office, 1909.

"The Conservation Commission and the Wildlife Conservation Program." In *State of Missouri: Official Manual for the Years Nineteen Thirty-Seven and Nineteen Thirty-Eight*, 555–62. Jefferson City: Secretary of State/Hugh Stephens Press, 1939.

Conway, Flaxen D. L., Pat Corcoran, and Greg Tillson. *Towns in Transition: Managing Change in Natural Resource Dependent Communities.* [Study guide to accompany video of the same name.] Corvallis: Oregon State University Extension Service, 1996.

Cunningham, Robert J. "River Drives: Driving logs downstream to the mill was a perilous part of logging activity." *Missouri Conservationist* 51, no. 9 (September 1990): 2–6.

———, and Carl Hauser. "The Decline of the Missouri Ozark Forest Between 1880 and 1920." In *Proceedings of Pine Hardwood Mixtures: A Symposium on Management and Ecology of the Type, Atlanta Georgia, April 18–19, 1989*, edited by Thomas A. Waldrop, 34–37. Asheville, NC: Southeastern Forest Experiment Station, 1989.

Denney, Hugh, ed. *A Regional Profile of the Ozark Foothills.* Columbia: University of Missouri, Extension Division, 1970.

Dunlap, Frederick. "Flora: Commercial Timber." In *The State of Missouri: Its Story, Chronology, Government, Climate, Ecology, Geology, Physiography, Flora, Fauna, Soil, Waters, Agriculture, Manufactures, Products, Transportation, Cities, Counties, People, Educational Institutions, Health, Recreation, Finances, Statistics, Citizens, and Enterprises, Together with Its Industries and Resources Natural and Created*, edited by H. R. Walmsley, 120–32. Kansas City, MO: Lewis Printing, 1932.

———. "Missouri's Development Through Forestry." In *State of Missouri: Official Manual for Years Nineteen Twenty-Five and Nineteen Twenty-Six*, 956–60. Jefferson City: Secretary of State, 1927.

Ensminger, Douglas, comp. "Handbook for Community Organizers and County Social Workers in Carter County." Columbia, MO: Missouri Relief and Reconstruction Commission, 1934.

Fickle, James E. *Mississippi Forests and Forestry.* Jackson: University Press of Mississippi, 2001.

Fine, Lisa M. *The Souls of the Skyscraper: Female Clerical Workers in Chicago, 1870–1930.* Philadelphia: Temple University Press, 1990.

Flader, Susan, ed. *Exploring Missouri's Legacy: State Parks and Historic Sites.* Columbia:

University of Missouri Press, 1992.

Folk, Joseph W. "Message: Waterways and Forestry." In *Appendix to the House and Senate Journals...1909*, pp. 13–18.

Galloway, John A. "John Barber White: Lumberman." PhD diss., University of Missouri–Columbia, 1961.

Gannett, Henry. *Report of the National Conservation Commission, February, 1909. Special message from the President of the United States transmitting a report of the National Conservation Commission, with accompanying papers*. Washington, DC: Government Printing Office, 1909.

Gerlach, Russel L. *Immigrants in the Ozarks: A Study in Ethnic Geography*. Columbia: University of Missouri Press, 1976.

———. *Settlement Patterns in Missouri: A Study of Population Origins with a Wall Map*. Columbia: University of Missouri Press, 1986.

Gibson, Jane W. "Living by the Land and Rivers of the Southeastern Missouri Ozarks." Draft copy of report submitted to National Park Service, Midwest Region, Lincoln, NE, 18 January 2000.

Gilmore, Robert K. *Ozark Baptizings, Hangings, and Other Diversions: Theatrical Folkways of Rural Missouri, 1885–1910*. Norman: University of Oklahoma Press, 1984.

Gough, Robert. *Farming the Cutover: A Social History of Northern Wisconsin, 1900–1940*. Lawrence: University Press of Kansas, 1997.

Gutman, Herbert G. *Work, Culture, and Society in Industrializing America: Essays in American Working-Class and Social History*. New York: Alfred A. Knopf, 1976.

Hadley, Herbert S. "Waterways and Forestry Commission, April 19, 1909." In *Appendix to the House and Senate Journals...1909*, sect. 6, pp. 3–7.

Hahn, Steven. "Common Right and Commonwealth: The Stock-Law Struggle and the Roots of Southern Populism." In *Region, Race, and Reconstruction: Essays in Honor of C. Vann Woodward*, edited by J. Morgan Kousser and James M. McPherson, 151–87. New York: Oxford University Press, 1982.

———. "The Roots of Southern Populism: Yeoman Farmers and the Transformation of Georgia's Upper Piedmont, 1850–1890." PhD diss., Yale University, 1979.

Hall, Jacqueline Dowd, et al. *Like a Family: The Making of a Southern Cotton Mill World*. Chapel Hill: University of North Carolina Press, 1987.

Hathaway, Thomas T. "Speech in favor of a stock law in Missouri delivered by the Hon. Thomas T. Hathaway, of St. Louis, March 1873, Twenty-seventh General Assembly—Regular Session." Jefferson City: Regan and Carter, State Printers, 1873.

Hays, Samuel P. *Conservation and the Gospel of Efficiency: The Progressive Conservation Movement, 1890–1920*. Cambridge, MA: Harvard University Press, 1959.

Hill, Leslie G. "History of the Missouri Lumber and Mining Company, 1880–1909." PhD diss., University of Missouri–Columbia, 1949.

Howard, W. L. "Missouri's Timber Supply." In *Missouri State Board of Horticulture, Annual Report for 1908*. Jefferson City, MO: Hugh Stephens Printing Co., 1909.

Hyde, Jr., Samuel C. *Pistols and Politics: The Dilemma of Democracy in Louisiana's Florida Parishes, 1810–1899*. Baton Rouge: Louisiana State University Press, 1996.

Janiewski, Dolores. "Southern Honor, Southern Dishonor: Managerial Ideology and the

Construction of Gender, Race, and Class Relations in Southern Industry." In *Work Engendered: Toward a New History of American Labor*, edited by Ava Baron, 70–81. Ithaca, NY: Cornell University Press, 1991.

Johnson, Paul E. *A Shopkeeper's Millennium: Society and Revivals in Rochester, New York, 1815–1837*. New York: Hill and Wang, 1978.

Johnson, Susan Lee. "Bulls, Bears, and Dancing Boys: Race, Gender, and Leisure in the California Gold Rush." In *Across the Great Divide: Cultures of Manhood in the American West*, edited by Matthew Basso, Laura McCall, and Dee Garceau, 45–72. New York: Routledge, 2001.

———. *Roaring Camp: The Social World of the California Gold Rush*. New York: W. W. Norton, 2000.

Kantor, Shawn Everett. *Politics and Property Rights: The Closing of the Open Range in the Postbellum South*. Chicago: University of Chicago Press, 1998.

Kaufman, Harold F. "Social Factors in the Reforestation of the Missouri Ozarks." Master's thesis, University of Missouri, 1939.

Keefe, James F. *The First 50 Years*. Jefferson City: Missouri Department of Conservation, 1987.

Kimmel, Michael. *Manhood in America: A Cultural History*. New York: Free Press, 1995.

Krusekopf, H. H., et al. *Soil Survey of Reynolds County, Missouri: Advance Sheets–Field Operations of the Bureau of Soils, 1918*. Washington, DC: Government Printing Office; U.S. Department of Agriculture, Bureau of Soils, 1921.

Kulik, Gary. "Dams, Fish, and Farmers: Defense of Public Rights in Eighteenth-Century Rhode Island." In *The Countryside in the Age of Capitalist Transformation: Essays in the Social History of Rural America*, edited by Steven Hahn and Jonathon Prude, 25–50. Chapel Hill: University of North Carolina Press, 1985.

Kwolek-Folland, Angel. "Gender, Self, and Work in the Life Insurance Industry, 1880–1930." In *Work Engendered: Toward a New History of American Labor*, edited by Ava Baron, 168–90. Ithaca, NY: Cornell University Press, 1991.

Lawrence, Robert, Bruce Moltzan, and Keith Moser. "Oak Decline and the Future of Missouri's Forests." (Brochure.) Jefferson City: Conservation Commission of Missouri, 2002.

Loveland, Lillian S. *Two Years in Grandin, 1896–1897: An Interesting Story of a Missouri Saw Mill Community; The Place and the People*. St. Louis: St. Louis Lumberman Print, n.d.

Marbut, Curtis F. "The Physical Features of Missouri." In *Reports of the Missouri Geological Survey*, 10:101–12. Jefferson City: Tribune Printing, State Printers and Binders, 1896.

———. "Soil Reconnaissance of the Ozark Region of Missouri and Arkansas." In U.S. Department of Agriculture, Bureau of Soils, *Field Operations of the Bureau of Soils, With Accompanying Papers by Assistants in Charge of Field Parties, 1911*, edited by Milton Whitney, 1727–1873. Washington, DC: Government Printing Office, 1911.

Marks, Stuart A. *Southern Hunting in Black and White: Nature, History, and Ritual in a Carolina Community*. Princeton, NJ: Princeton University Press, 1991.

Marquis, Albert Nelson. *The Book of St. Louisans: A Biographical Dictionary of the Leading Living Men of the City of St. Louis and Vicinity, 1912*. St. Louis: St. Louis Republic, 1912.

Massey, Ellen Gray, ed. *Bittersweet Country*. Garden City, NY: Anchor Press, 1978.

McCanse, Keith. *Annual Report of the State Game and Fish Commissioner of the State of Missouri for the Year Ending December 31, 1925, to the Honorable Sam A. Baker, Governor of Missouri.* Jefferson City: Hugh Stephens Printing, 1926.

McManus, Thelma S., comp. *Grandin (Carter) Missouri Records, 1880–1912.* Doniphan, MO: n.p., 1984.

McMath, Robert C., Jr. "Sandy Land and Hogs in the Timber: (Agri)cultural Origins of the Farmers' Alliance in Texas." In *The Countryside in the Age of Capitalist Transformation: Essays in the Social History of Rural America,* edited by Steven Hahn and Jonathan Prude, 205–27. Chapel Hill: University of North Carolina Press, 1985.

McWhiney, Grady, and Forest McDonald. "Celtic Origins of Southern Herding Practices." *Journal of Southern History* 51, no. 2 (May 1985): 165–82.

Meier, Calvin Edmund. "The Effect of Fire on Hardwood Forest Soil of the Missouri Ozarks." Master's thesis, University of Missouri–Columbia, 1974.

Missouri Bureau of Labor Statistics. *Annual Report* [annual publication]. Jefferson City: Missouri Bureau of Labor Statistics, 1897, 1901, and 1904.

Missouri Conservation Commission. *Annual Report of the Missouri Conservation Commission, the Organization, Policies, and Activities for the Year 1942.* Jefferson City: Mid-State Printing Co., 1943.

———. *Annual Report of the Missouri Conservation Commission, the Organization, Policies, and Activities for the Year 1944.* Jefferson City: Mid-State Printing Co., 1945.

Missouri Department of Conservation, State Fire Marshall. *Living With Wildfire.* Pamphlet no. F0013, January 2002.

"Missouri Forests." In *State of Missouri: Official Manual for the Years Nineteen Forty-Five and Nineteen Forty-Six,* 664–65. Jefferson City: Secretary of State/Hugh Stephens Press, 1947.

Missouri State Gazetteer and Business Directory for 1893–1894. St. Louis: R. L. Polk and Co., 1893.

Missouri State Gazetteer for 1898. St. Louis: R. L. Polk and Co., 1898.

Montgomery, David. *Workers' Control in America: Studies in the History of Work, Technology, and Labor Struggles.* Cambridge: Cambridge University Press, 1979.

Morrison, Kathleen. "The Poverty of Place: A Comparative Study of Five Rural Counties in the Missouri Ozarks." PhD diss., University of Missouri–Columbia, 1999.

Morrow, Lynn. *Shepherd of the Hills: Tourism Transforms the Ozarks, 1880s–1930s.* Fayetteville: University of Arkansas Press, 1999.

Murphy, Mary. *Mining Cultures: Men, Women, and Leisure in Butte, 1914–41.* Urbana: University of Illinois Press, 1997.

"New Forestry Division." In *State of Missouri: Official Manual for Years Nineteen Twenty-Five and Nineteen Twenty-Six,* 828–959. Jefferson City: Secretary of State/Hugh Stephens Press, 1927.

Oakley, Eugene. *The Deserted Village: A History of Grandin, Missouri.* N.p., 1968.

———. *A History of Grandin and the Missouri Lumber and Mining Company.* N.p., 1963.

Official Manual of the State of Missouri for the Years 1899–1900. Jefferson City: Secretary of State/Tribune Publishing, 1900.

Ownby, Ted. *Subduing Satan: Religion, Recreation, and Manhood in the Rural South, 1865–*

1920. Chapel Hill: University of North Carolina Press, 1993.

Peck, Gunther. "Manly Gambles: The Politics of Risk on the Comstock Lode, 1860–1880." In *Across the Great Divide: Cultures of Manhood in the American West,* edited by Matthew Basso, Laura McCall, and Dee Garceau, 73–96. New York: Routledge, 2001.

Ponder, Jerry. *Grandin, Hunter, and West Eminence and the Missouri Lumber and Mining Company.* Doniphan, MO: Ponder Books, 1989.

Price, Jim (NPS archaeologist, Ozark National Scenic Riverways, Van Buren, MO). "Ozark Experiences." Handouts from lecture, ca. 2002.

Pudup, Mary Beth, Dwight B. Billings, and Altina L. Waller. *Appalachia in the Making: The Mountain South in the Nineteenth Century.* Chapel Hill: University of North Carolina Press, 1995.

Pyne, Stephen. *Fire in America: A Cultural History of Wildland and Rural Fire.* Princeton, NJ: Princeton University Press, 1982.

Rafferty, Milton D. *The Ozarks: Land and Life.* Norman: University of Oklahoma Press, 1980.

Randolph, Vance. *Ozark Mountain Folks.* New York: Vanguard Press, 1932.

Rayburn, Otto Ernest. *Ozark Country.* New York: Duell, Sloan & Pearce, 1941.

Record, Samuel J. "Missouri's Opportunities in Forestry." In *Missouri State Board of Agriculture Annual Report, 1908,* 1–9. Jefferson City: Hugh Stephens Printing, 1909.

A Reminiscent History of the Ozarks Region (1894). In the Center for Ozark Studies Collection, Record Group 8.11, Department of Special Collections and Archives, Duane G. Meyer Library, Missouri State University, Springfield, MO.

Report on Forest Conditions to Joint Congressional Committee on Forestry. Washington, DC: Government Printing Office, 1938.

"Report of the Forestry Division." In *State of Missouri: Official Manual for the Years Nineteen Forty-Seven and Nineteen Forty-Eight,* 279–82. Jefferson City: Secretary of State/Hugh Stephens Press, 1949.

"Report of the Forestry Division." In *State of Missouri: Official Manual for the Years Nineteen Thirty-One and Nineteen Thirty-Two,* 626–27. Jefferson City: Secretary of State/Hugh Stephens Press, 1929.

"Report of the Forestry Division." In *State of Missouri: Official Manual for the Years Nineteen Twenty-Seven and Nineteen Twenty-Eight,* 662–64. Jefferson City: Secretary of State/ Hugh Stephens Press, 1929.

"Report of the Forestry Division." In *State of Missouri: Official Manual for the Years Nineteen Twenty-Nine and Nineteen Thirty,* 816–19. Jefferson City: Secretary of State/Hugh Stephens Press, 1929.

Robinson, Glen O. *The Forest Service: A Study in Public Land Management.* Baltimore: Johns Hopkins University Press, 1975.

Rodes, J. H. *Annual Report of the State Game and Fish Warden of the State of Missouri for the Year Ending December 31, 1905, to the Hon. Joseph Folk, Governor of Missouri.* Jefferson City: Hugh Stephens Printing Co., 1906.

———. *Annual Report of the State Game and Fish Warden of the State of Missouri for the Year Ending December 31, 1907, to the Hon. Joseph Folk, Governor of Missouri, Printed by Authority of the Walmsley Law of 1905.* Jefferson City: Hugh Stephens Printing Co., 1908.

Rosenzweig, Roy. *Eight Hours for What We Will: Workers and Leisure in an Industrial City,*

1870–1920. Cambridge: Cambridge University Press, 1983.

Ross, John H., State Game and Fish Commissioner. *Annual Report of the State Game and Fish Commissioner to the Honorable Guy B. Park, Governor of the State of Missouri, For the Year Ending December 31, 1932.* Jefferson City: Hugh Stephens Printing Co., 1932.

Sauer, Carl O. *The Geography of the Ozark Highland of Missouri.* Chicago: University of Chicago Press, 1920.

Schiff, Ashley L. *Fire and Water: Scientific Heresy in the Forest Service.* Cambridge, MA: Harvard University Press, 1962.

Schmidt, Thomas L. "Missouri's Forest Resources in 1999." U.S. Department of Agriculture, Research Note RN-NC-375. St. Paul, MN: U.S. Forest Service, North Central Research Station, 1999.

Schultz, Gerard. "Missouri and the War, Part XVI." *Missouri Historical Review* 40, no. 4 (July 1946): 531–45.

Scott, Anne Firor. *Natural Allies: Women's Associations in American History.* Urbana: University of Illinois Press, 1991.

Scowcroft, Paul G. "The Effects of Fire on the Hardwood Forests of the Missouri Ozarks." Master's thesis, University of Missouri–Columbia, 1966.

Spencer, Jr., John S., Sue M. Roussopoulos, and Robert Massengale. *Missouri's Forest Resource, 1989: An Analysis.* North Central Experiment Station, U.S. Forest Service, U.S. Department of Agriculture, Resource Bulletin NC-139, 1992.

Stepenoff, Bonnie. *Big Spring Autumn.* Kirksville, MO: Truman State University Press, 2008.

Stevens, Donald L. *A Homeland and A Hinterland: The Current and Jacks Fork Riverways, Historic Resource Study, Ozark National Scenic Riverways.* Omaha, NE: National Park Service, Midwest Region, 1991.

Steyermark, Julian A. *Vegetational History of the Ozark Forest.* Columbia: University of Missouri Studies, 1959.

Thelen, David. *Paths of Resistance: Tradition and Democracy in Industrializing Missouri.* Columbia: University of Missouri Press, 1986.

Theobald, Robert. *The Rapids of Change: Social Entrepreneurship in Turbulent Times.* Indianapolis: Knowledge Systems, 1987.

Tolerton, Jesse A. *First Annual Report of the State Game and Fish Commissioner of the State of Missouri for the Year Ending December 31, 1909, to the Honorable Herbert S. Hadley, Governor of Missouri.* Jefferson City: Hugh Stephens Printing, 1910.

Trotter, Joe William, Jr. *Coal, Class, and Color: Blacks in Southern West Virginia, 1915–32.* Urbana: University of Illinois Press, 1990.

U.S. Bureau of the Census. *Thirteenth Census of the United States, Taken in the Year 1910.* Washington, DC: Government Printing Office, 1913.

U.S. Bureau of the Census. *Twelfth Census of the United States, Taken in the Year 1900.* Washington, DC: Government Printing Office, 1902.

U.S. Census Office. *1870 U.S. Census Population Schedules.* Washington, DC: Government Printing Office, 1870.

U.S. Federal Security Agency [McEntee, J. J.]. *Final Report of the Director of the Civilian Conservation Corps, April 1933–June 30, 1942.* [Washington, DC]: U.S. Federal Security Agency, 1942.

Von Schrenk, "Report of the Missouri Forestry Commission." In *Appendix to the House and Senate Journals...1909,* sect. 48, pp. 3–8.

Warren, Louis S. *The Hunter's Game: Poachers and Conservationists in Twentieth-Century America.* New Haven, CT: Yale University Press, 1997.

Westin, Steve, comp., "Wildfire in Missouri." Missouri Department of Conservation, July 1992.

Westveld, Ruthford H. *Applied Silviculture in the United States.* Ann Arbor, MI: Edwards Brothers, 1935.

———. *History of Forestry at the University of Missouri–Columbia.* Special Report 120. Columbia: University of Missouri–Columbia Agricultural Experiment Station, 1970.

Williams, John Alexander. *Appalachia: A History.* Chapel Hill: University of North Carolina Press, 2002.

Williams, Michael. *Americans and Their Forests: A Historical Geography.* Cambridge: Cambridge University Press, 1989.

Woodruff, Stephen. "William H. Black: Missouri Leader in the Ecumenical Movement." *Missouri Historical Review* 67, no. 1 (October 1972): 75–97.

About the Author

David Benac received his doctorate degree from the University of Missouri where he specialized in environmental and social history. He is currently an associate professor of history at Southeastern Louisiana University with research and teaching fields in public and environmental history. He has published in the Missouri Historical Review, Big Muddy, and Journal of the Mississippi River Valley, and has published widely in federal studies of historical preservation.

Index